W9-AFM-433

Grades K–2

THE SUPER SOURCE®

Pattern Blocks

ETA/Cuisenaire®
Vernon Hills, IL

ETA/Cuisenaire® extends its warmest thanks to the many teachers and students across the country who helped ensure the success of The SUPER SOURCE® series by participating in the outlining, writing, and field testing of the materials.

Project Director: Judith Adams
Managing Editor: Doris Hirschhorn
Editorial Team: John Nelson, Deborah J. Slade, Harriet Slonim
Field Test Coordinator: Laurie Verdeschi

Design Manager: Phyllis Aycock
Text Design: Amy Berger, Tracey Munz
Line Art and Production: Joan Lee, Fiona Santoianni
Cover Design: Stacy Tisci, David Jensen
Illustrations: Sean Farrell

The SUPER SOURCE® Pattern Blocks Grades K–2
ETA 75381
ISBN 978-1-57452-009-5

ETA/Cuisenaire • Vernon Hills, IL 60061-1862
800-445-5985 • www.etacuisenaire.com

© 2007, 1996 by ETA/Cuisenaire®
All rights reserved.

No part of this publication may be reproduced, stored in a retrieval system, or transmitted, in any form or by any means, electronic, mechanical, photocopying, recording, or otherwise, without the prior written permission of the publisher. Permission is granted for limited reproduction of pages 90–104 of this book for classroom use and not for resale.

Printed in the United States of America.

07 08 09 10 11 12 13 14 15 16   10 9 8 7 6 5 4 3 2 1

Table of Contents

Using THE SUPER SOURCE®

The Super Source™ is a series of books, each of which contains a collection of activities to use with a specific math manipulative. Driving **the Super Source**™ is Cuisenaire's conviction that children construct their own understandings through rich, hands-on mathematical experiences. Although the activities in each book are written for a specific grade range, they all connect to the core of mathematics learning that is important to every K-6 child. Thus, the material in many activities can easily be refocused for children at other grade levels. Because the activities are not arranged sequentially, children can work on any activity at any time.

The lessons in **the Super Source**™ all follow a basic structure consistent with the vision of mathematics teaching described in the *Curriculum and Evaluation Standards for School Mathematics* published by the National Council of Teachers of Mathematics.

All of the activities in this series involve Problem Solving, Communication, Reasoning, and Mathematical Connections—the first four NCTM Standards. Each activity also focuses on one or more of the following curriculum strands: Number, Geometry, Measurement, Patterns/Functions, Probability/Statistics, Logic.

HOW LESSONS ARE ORGANIZED

At the beginning of each lesson, you will find, to the right of the title, both the major curriculum strands to which the lesson relates and the particular topics that children will work with. Each lesson has three main sections. The first, GETTING READY, offers an *Overview*, which states what children will be doing, and why, and provides a list of "What You'll Need." Specific numbers of Pattern Blocks are suggested on this list but can be adjusted as the needs of your specific situation dictate. Before an activity, blocks can be counted out and placed in containers or self-sealing plastic bags for easy distribution. When crayons are called for, it is understood that their colors are those that match the Pattern Blocks and that markers may be used in place of crayons. Blackline masters that are provided for your convenience at the back of the book are also referenced on this materials list. Paper, pencils, scissors, tape, and materials for making charts, which may be necessary in certain activities, are usually not.

Although overhead Pattern Blocks are always listed in "What You'll Need" as optional, these materials are highly effective when you want to demonstrate the use of Pattern Blocks. As you move blocks on the screen, children can work with the same materials at their seats. If overhead Pattern Blocks are not available, you may want to make and use transparencies of the Pattern Block shapes (see page 98). Children can also use the overhead Pattern Blocks and/or a transparency of the triangle paper to present their work to other members of their group or to the class.

The second section, THE ACTIVITY, first presents a possible scenario for *Introducing* the children to the activity. The aim of this brief introduction is to help you give children the tools they will need to investigate independently. However, care has been taken to avoid undercutting the activity itself. Since these investigations are designed to enable children to increase their own mathematical power, the idea is to set the stage but not steal the show! The heart of the lesson, *On Their Own*, is found in a box at the top of the second page of each lesson. Here, rich problems stimulate many different problem-solving approaches and lead to a variety of solutions. These hands-on explorations have the potential for bringing children to new mathematical ideas and deepening skills.

©ETA/Cuisenaire®

On Their Own is intended as a stand-alone activity for children to explore with a partner or in a small group. Be sure to make the needed directions clearly visible. You may want to write them on the chalkboard or on an overhead or present them either on reusable cards or paper. For children who may have difficulty reading the directions, you can read them aloud or make sure that at least one "reader" is in each group.

The last part of this second section, *The Bigger Picture*, gives suggestions for how children can share their work and their thinking and make mathematical connections. Class charts and children's recorded work provide a springboard for discussion. Under "Thinking and Sharing," there are several prompts that you can use to promote discussion. Children will not be able to respond to these prompts with one-word answers. Instead, the prompts encourage children to describe what they notice, tell how they found their results, and give the reasoning behind their answers. Thus children learn to verify their own results rather than relying on the teacher to determine if an answer is "right" or "wrong." Though the class discussion might immediately follow the investigation, it is important not to cut the activity short by having a class discussion too soon.

The Bigger Picture often includes a suggestion for a "Writing" (or drawing) assignment. This is meant to help children process what they have just been doing. You might want to use these ideas as a focus for daily or weekly entries in a math journal that each child keeps.

If there are things sticking out of your disighn. For a sampee say like rombasas and trapizoys and hexogans your ant will have to walk ferther.

From: *Ant Walks*

I took 12 Pattern Blocks. I had 3 Since dimins and 3 Trapazoeys they fided. The dimins had 1 more Thean The Sqars

From: *Scoop and Sort*

The Bigger Picture always ends with ideas for "Extending the Activity." Extensions take the essence of the main activity and either alter or extend its parameters. These activities are well used with a class that becomes deeply involved in the primary activity or for children who finish before the others. In any case, it is probably a good idea to expose the entire class to the possibility of, and the results from, such extensions.

The third and final section of the lesson is TEACHER TALK. Here, in *Where's the Mathematics?*, you can gain insight into the underlying mathematics of the activity and discover some of the strategies children are apt to use as they work. Solutions are also given— when such are necessary and/or helpful. Because *Where's the Mathematics?* provides a view of what may happen in the lesson as well as the underlying mathematical potential that may grow out of it, this may be the section that you want to read before presenting the activity to children.

USING THE ACTIVITIES

The Super Source™ has been designed to fit into the variety of classroom environments in which it will be used. These range from a completely manipulative-based classroom to one in which manipulatives are just beginning to play a part. You may choose to use some activities in *the Super Source*™ in the way set forth in each lesson (introducing an activity to the whole class, then breaking the class up into groups that all work on the same task, and so forth). You will then be able to circulate among the groups as they work to observe and perhaps comment on each child's work. This approach requires a full classroom set of materials but allows you to concentrate on the variety of ways that children respond to a given activity.

Alternatively, you may wish to make two or three related activities available to different groups of children at the same time. You may even wish to use different manipulatives to explore the same mathematical concept. (Geoboards and Tangrams, for example, can be used to teach some of the same geometric principles as Pattern Blocks.) This approach does not require full classroom sets of a particular manipulative. It also permits greater adaptation of materials to individual children's needs and/or preferences.

If children are comfortable working independently, you might want to set up a "menu"—that is, set out a number of related activities from which children can choose. Children should be encouraged to write about their experiences with these independent activities.

However you choose to use *the Super Source*™ activities, it would be wise to allow time for several groups or the entire class to share their experiences. The dynamics of this type of interaction, where children share not only solutions and strategies but also feelings and intuitions, is the basis of continued mathematical growth. It allows children who are beginning to form a mathematical structure to clarify it and those who have mastered just isolated concepts to begin to see how these concepts might fit together.

Again, both the individual teaching style and combined learning styles of the children should dictate the specific method of utilizing *the Super Source*™ lessons. At first sight, some activities may appear too difficult for some of your children, and you may find yourself tempted to actually "teach" by modeling exactly how an activity can lead to a particular learning outcome. If you do this, you rob children of the chance to try the activity in whatever way they can. As long as children have a way to begin an investigation, give them time and opportunity to see it through. Instead of making assumptions about what children will or won't do, watch and listen. The excitement and challenge of the activity—as well as the chance to work cooperatively—may bring out abilities in children that will surprise you.

If you are convinced, however, that an activity does not suit your students, adjust it, by all means. You may want to change the language, either by simplifying it or by referring to specific vocabulary that you and your children already use and are comfortable with. On the other hand, if you suspect that an activity isn't challenging enough, you may want to read through the activity extensions for a variation that you can give children instead.

RECORDING

Although the direct process of working with Pattern Blocks is a valuable one, it is afterward, when children look at, compare, share, and think about their constructions, that an activity yields its greatest rewards. However, because Pattern Block designs can't always be left intact for very long, children need an effective way to record their work. To this end, at the back of this book recording paper is provided for reproduction. The "What You'll Need" listing

 ©ETA/Cuisenaire®

at the beginning of each lesson often specifies the kind of recording paper to use. For example, in an activity where children are working with only the yellow, red, blue, and green Pattern Blocks, they can duplicate their work or trace the Pattern Block pieces on the Pattern Block triangle paper found on page 91.

When they also work with the orange and/or tan Pattern Blocks, children need a plain piece of recording paper, since these Pattern Block pieces don't fit neatly onto the triangle paper.

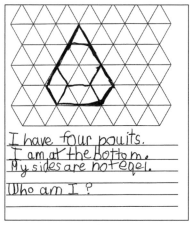

From: *Who Am I?*

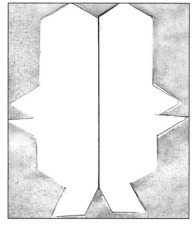

From: *Copy Cat*

From: *Cover the Caterpillar*

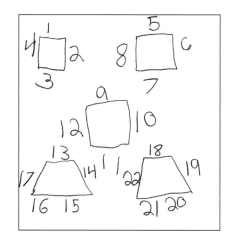

From: *How Many Seats?*

In this latter case, the children will have to find a way to transfer their Pattern Block designs. They might choose to trace each Pattern Block piece in the design onto the plain paper or to use a Pattern Block template to reproduce each piece in the design. Templates of the exact size and shape of the Pattern Blocks can be bought or made from plastic coffee-can lids.

When young children explore Pattern Blocks, they are likely to use up every available block in making a huge pattern. This makes the pattern daunting to copy. Such patterns may be recorded using cutouts of the Pattern Block shapes (see page 98). Children can color the shapes and paste them in place on white paper.

Another interesting way to "freeze" a Pattern Block design is to create it using a software piece, such as *Shape Up!*, and then get a printout. Children can use a classroom or resource-room computer if it is available or, where possible, extend the activity into a home assignment by utilizing their home computers.

Recording involves more than copying the designs. Writing, drawing, and making charts and tables are also ways to record. By creating a table of data gathered in the course of their investigations, children are able to draw conclusions and look for patterns. When children write or draw, either in their group or later by themselves, they are clarifying their understanding of their recent mathematical experience.

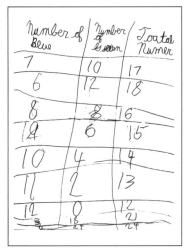

From: *Cover the Caterpillar*

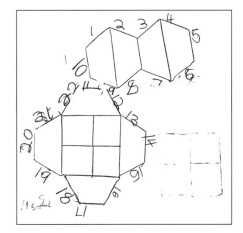

From: *Things with Legs*

From: *Pattern Block Toy Factory*

From: *How Many Seats?*

With a roomful of children busily engaged in their investigations, it is not easy for a teacher to keep track of how individual children are working. Having tangible material to gather and examine when the time is right will help you to keep in close touch with each child's learning.

©ETA/Cuisenaire®

Exploring Pattern Blocks

A set of Pattern Blocks consists of blocks in six geometric, color-coded shapes, referred to as: green triangles, orange squares, blue parallelograms, tan rhombuses, red trapezoids, and yellow hexagons. The relationships among the side measures and among the angle measures make it very easy to fit the blocks together to make tiling patterns which completely cover a flat surface. The blocks are designed so that all the sides of the shapes are 1 inch except the longer side of the trapezoid, which is 2 inches, or twice as long as the other sides. Except for the tan rhombus, which has two angles that measure 150°, all of the shapes have angles whose measures are divisors of 360—120°, 90°, 60°, and 30°. Yet even these 150° angles relate to the other angles, since 150° is the sum of 90° and 60°.

Green triangle   Orange square   Blue parallelogram   Tan rhombus   Red trapezoid   Yellow hexagon
(rhombus)

These features of the Pattern Blocks encourage investigation of relationships among the shapes. One special aspect of the shapes is that the yellow block can be covered exactly by putting together two red blocks, or three blue blocks, or six green blocks. This is a natural lead-in to the consideration of how fractional parts relate to a whole—the yellow block. Thus, when children work only with the yellow, red, blue, and green blocks, and the yellow block is chosen as the unit, then a red block represents 1/2, a blue block represents 1/3, and a green block represents 1/6. Within this small world of fractions, children can develop hands-on familiarity and intuition about comparing fractions, finding equivalent fractions, changing improper fractions to mixed numbers, and modeling addition, subtraction, division, and multiplication of fractions.

Pattern Blocks provide a visual image which is essential for real understanding of fraction algorithms. Many children learn to do examples such as "3 1/2 = ?/2," "1/2 x 1/3 = ?" or 4 ÷ 1/3 = ?" at a purely symbolic level so that if they forget the procedure, they are at a total loss. Yet children who have had many presymbolic experiences solving problems such as "Find how many red blocks fit over three yellows and a red," "Find half of the blue block," or "Find how many blue blocks cover four yellow blocks" will have a solid intuitive foundation on which to build these skills and to fall back on if memory fails them.

reds 5
Blues 5
Greens 5
altogether fifteen
3's with 10 more
I counted by 3 intill I got 5 more

From: *Pattern Block Walls*

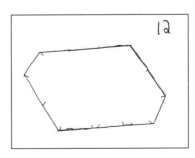

From: *Ant Walks*

Children do need ample time to experiment freely with Pattern Blocks, however, before they begin more serious investigations. Most children can begin without additional direction, but some may need suggestions. Asking children to find the different shapes, sizes, and colors of Pattern Blocks, or asking them to cover their desktops with the blocks or to find which blocks can be used to build straight roads, might be good for "starters."

WORKING WITH PATTERN BLOCKS

As children begin to work with Pattern Blocks, they use them primarily to explore spatial relations. Young children have an initial tendency to work with others and to copy one another's designs. Yet even duplicating another's pattern with blocks can expand a child's experience, develop ability to recognize similarities and differences, and provide a context for developing language related to geometric ideas. Throughout their investigations, children should be encouraged to talk about their constructions. Expressing their thoughts out loud helps children to clarify and extend their thinking.

Pattern Blocks help children to explore many mathematical topics, including congruence, similarity, symmetry, area, perimeter, patterns, functions, fractions, and graphing. The following are just a few of the possibilities:

When playing "exchange games" with the various sized blocks, children can develop an understanding of relationships between objects with different values, such as coins or place-value models.

When trying to identify which blocks can be put together to make another shape, children can begin to build a base for the concept of fractional pieces.

When the blocks are used to completely fill in an outline, the concept of area is developed. If children explore measuring the same area using different blocks as units they can develop understandings about the relationship of the size of the unit and the measure of the area.

When investigating the perimeter of shapes made with Pattern Blocks, children can discover that shapes with the same area can have different perimeters and that shapes with the same perimeter can have different areas.

When using Pattern Blocks to cover a flat surface, children can discover that some combinations of corners, or angles, fit together or can be arranged around a point. Knowing that a full circle measures 360° enables children to find the various angle measurements.

When finding how many blocks of the same color it takes to make a larger shape similar to the original block (which can be done with all but the yellow hexagon), children can discover the square number pattern—1, 4, 9, 16, ...

I think the 14 Units is better because he gets More exrisise

From: *Ant Walks*

ASSESSING CHILDREN'S UNDERSTANDING

The use of Pattern Blocks provides a perfect opportunity for authentic assessment. Watching children work with the blocks gives you a sense of how they approach a mathematical problem. Their thinking can be "seen" through their positioning of the Pattern Blocks. When a class breaks up into small working groups, you are able to circulate, listen, and raise questions, all the while focusing on how individuals are thinking.

The challenges that children encounter when working with Pattern Blocks often elicit unexpected abilities from children whose performance in more symbolic, number-oriented tasks may be weak. On the other hand, some children with good memories for numerical relationships have difficulty with spatial challenges and can more readily learn from freely exploring with Pattern Blocks. Thus, by observing children's free exploration, you can get a sense of individual styles and intellectual strengths.

Having children describe their creations and share their strategies and thinking with the whole class gives you another opportunity for observational assessment. Furthermore, you may want to gather children's recorded work or invite them to choose pieces to add to their math portfolios.

From: *Red, Green, or Yellow*

From: *Three in a Row*

Models of teachers assessing children's understanding can be found in Cuisenaire's series of videotapes listed below.

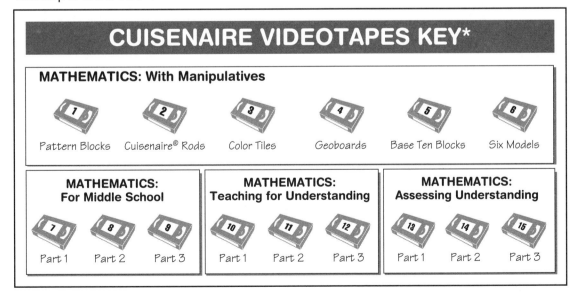

*See *Overview of the Lessons*, pages 16–17, for specific lesson/video correlation.

Connect THE SUPER SOURCE® to NCTM Standards.

STRANDS

	PROBLEM SOLVING	COMMUNICATION	REASONING	CONNECTIONS	Geometry	Logic	Measurement	Number	Patterns/Functions	Probability/Statistics
ANTWALKS	◆	◆	◆	◆	◆		◆			
CLOSEST TO THE FINISH LINE	◆	◆	◆	◆		◆				◆
COPY CAT	◆	◆	◆	◆	◆					
COVER THE CATERPILLAR	◆	◆						◆	◆	
HOW MANY SEATS?	◆	◆	◆	◆	◆			◆	◆	
LOOK HOW I'M GROWING	◆	◆	◆	◆					◆	
ONE HUNDRED	◆	◆	◆	◆	◆		◆	◆		
PATTERN BLOCK PIZZA	◆	◆	◆	◆	◆					◆
PATTERN BLOCK TOY FACTORY	◆	◆		◆	◆			◆		
PATTERN BLOCK WALLS	◆	◆	◆	◆	◆			◆	◆	
RED, GREEN, OR YELLOW?	◆	◆		◆			◆	◆		
SCOOP AND SORT	◆	◆	◆	◆				◆		◆
SPIN AND GRAPH	◆	◆	◆	◆						◆
SPIN TO WIN	◆	◆	◆	◆	◆	◆				
THINGS WITH LEGS	◆	◆	◆	◆	◆	◆		◆		
THREE IN A ROW	◆	◆	◆	◆	◆	◆				
WHO AM I?	◆	◆	◆	◆	◆	◆				
WHO CAUGHT THE BIGGER FISH?	◆	◆	◆	◆	◆		◆			

TOPICS

Correlate THE SUPER SOURCE® to your curriculum.

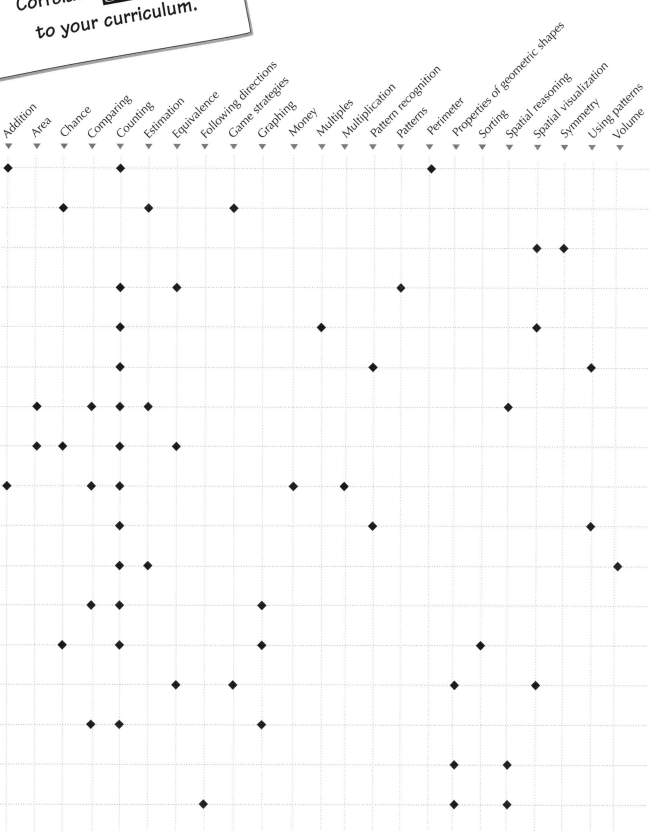

More THE SUPER SOURCE at a glance:
PATTERN BLOCKS for Grades 3-4 and Grades 5-6

Classroom-tested activities contained in these *Super Source*™ Pattern Blocks books focus on the math strands in the charts below.

THE SUPER SOURCE® Pattern Blocks, Grades 3–4

Geometry	Logic	Measurement
Number	**Patterns/Functions**	**Probability/Statistics**

THE SUPER SOURCE® Pattern Blocks, Grades 5–6

Geometry	Logic	Measurement
Number	**Patterns/Functions**	**Probability/Statistics**

More THE SUPER SOURCE® at a glance:
ADDITIONAL MANIPULATIVES and Grades K–2

Classroom-tested activities contained in these *Super Source*™ books focus on the math strands as indicated in these charts.

THE SUPER SOURCE® Snap Cubes®, Grades K-2

Geometry	Logic	Measurement
Number	Patterns/Functions	Probability/Statistics

THE SUPER SOURCE® Cuisenaire Rods®, Grades K-2

Geometry	Logic	Measurement
Number	Patterns/Functions	Probability/Statistics

THE SUPER SOURCE® Geoboards, Grades K-2

Geometry	Logic	Measurement
Number	Patterns/Functions	Probability/Statistics

THE SUPER SOURCE® Color Tiles, Grades K-2

Geometry	Logic	Measurement
Number	Patterns/Functions	Probability/Statistics

THE SUPER SOURCE® Tangrams, Grades K-2

Geometry	Logic	Measurement
Number	Patterns/Functions	Probability/Statistics

©ETA/Cuisenaire®.

Overview of the Lessons

 See video key, page 11.

Pattern Blocks, Grades K-2

 See video key, page 11.

ANTWALKS

Getting Ready

What You'll Need

Pattern Blocks, 2 red, 2 blue, 2 yellow and 1 green per pair

Overhead Pattern Blocks (optional)

Overview

Children use a prescribed set of Pattern Blocks to create shapes around which an ant could walk. They then measure the length of the antwalks. In this activity, children have the opportunity to:

◆ find perimeter

◆ work with non-standard units

◆ construct shapes with the same area but different perimeters

The Activity

Be sure to call attention to how two triangles fit along the longer side of the trapezoid.

Introducing

◆ Show a red Pattern Block. Run your finger around the edges of the block and ask children to imagine that what you are tracing is a walking path for an ant.

◆ Ask volunteers for ideas on how to measure the length of the antwalk.

◆ Show children a green triangle. Establish that all three sides are the same length and that the antwalk around this block would be 3 units.

◆ Place green triangles around the red trapezoid. Have children count with you to demonstrate that the length of the antwalk around the red Pattern Block is 5 units.

◆ Have children use green triangles or paper cutouts of green triangles to find the length of the antwalk around another Pattern Block.

1 + 1 + 1 + 1 + 1
length of antwalk = 5

©ETA/Cuisenaire®

On Their Own

How many antwalks of different lengths can you design for an ant who is training for the Ant Olympics?

Antwalk

- Work with a partner.

- Get 2 red, 2 blue, and 2 yellow Pattern Blocks. Make an antwalk from these blocks. Here is a picture of what an antwalk can look like.

- Make sure that at least 1 complete side of each block touches a complete side of another block.

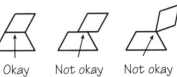
Okay   Not okay   Not okay

- Also, make sure that the blocks in your shape do not surround any empty spaces.

- Trace the shape of your antwalk on paper.

- Use an edge of a green block to find out how long the antwalk is. Write that number next to the picture of the antwalk.

- Use the same 6 blocks to make another antwalk. Make this antwalk longer or shorter than your first.

- Trace your new antwalk and record its length.

The Bigger Picture

Thinking and Sharing

Call on volunteers to share their designs with the class and tell how long each antwalk is. Post children's shapes.

Use prompts like these to promote class discussion:

- How are these antwalks the same? How are they different?
- Did anyone have a shorter path? Show it and explain.
- Did anyone have a longer path? Show it and explain.
- All of these paths are 12 units long and all of these are 20 units long. How are the shapes with the longer paths different from the shapes with shorter paths?
- Which antwalk do you think an ant should use most often to train for the Ant Olympics? Why?

Drawing and Writing

1. Ask older children to write down or draw the 10 Pattern Blocks they would select from the entire set of Pattern Blocks if they wanted to make a long training path. Ask them to tell why they chose those blocks.

2. Have children draw a picture of their favorite antwalk without showing the individual blocks. Have a partner predict the length of the path and then fill in the outline with Pattern Blocks and check the prediction.

Extending the Activity

1. Have children make a graph of their training paths grouping them by length. Discuss which length was most common and which was least common.

2. Have the children select their own set of Pattern Blocks and try to make a training path that is between 24 and 30 units long.

Teacher Talk

Where's the Mathematics?

In this activity, children discover that even though the same number and kind of Pattern Blocks may be used (area), the length of the antwalk (perimeter) can vary depending on how compactly the blocks are arranged.

Using 2 red, 2 blue, and 2 yellow Pattern Blocks, children will be able to make a variety of paths in five different lengths, namely 12, 14, 16, 18, or 20 units. All of these perimeters are even numbers. This evenness follows from the fact that the perimeters of the 6 individual blocks total 30 units (5 + 5 + 4 + 4 + 6 + 6 = 30). When two blocks are placed together to share a side, two sides—one from each block—are no longer part of the perimeter. As more blocks are placed together, the perimeter keeps being reduced by multiples of 2 and thus remains an even number.

The more compact the arrangement of the blocks, the smaller the perimeter of the shape. For example, here are two antwalks that each have a perimeter of 12 units.

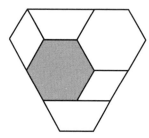 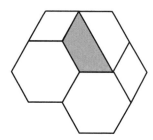

The shapes are compact in the sense that each block touches 2 or more other blocks. In fact, the shaded block in the first arrangement touches all 5 of the other pieces!

As the blocks are arranged in a more elongated fashion, so that each block touches fewer other blocks, the perimeter increases. Finally, when every block only touches one or two other blocks, the maximum perimeter of 20 units is reached.

©ETA/Cuisenaire®

3. Have children figure out the total distance an ant would walk if it walked on every one of the paths they created.

4. Have children find how long it would take an ant to walk on their paths if the ant can walk one unit of length in two seconds.

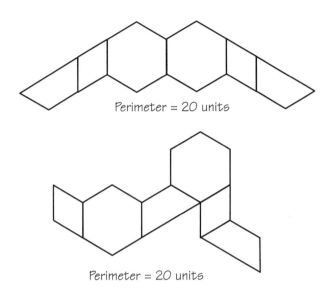

Perimeter = 20 units

Perimeter = 20 units

Children may not notice differences in shape as a perimeter moves from 12 to 14 units or from 14 to 16 units, but they will be able to note how compact the shapes are when they are presented with several examples of perimeters of 12 units all at once and then asked to contrast those shapes with the shapes with a perimeter of 20 units.

When asking children which antwalk should be used most often for an ant who is in training, you are asking them an optimization problem, a problem that has many solutions which must be sorted through to find an optimum or best solution in a particular situation. One child might pick the longest path so that the ant has a long practice time. Another might suggest that the shortest path is best because the ant could walk it twice and have more training than on the longest path. Still another child might select a training path because "the shape is interesting and the ant won't get bored." It's important for children to think about numerical solutions in context to the problem they are supposed to be solving. Math is most interesting when it is applied and not theoretical.

CLOSEST TO THE FINISH LINE

- **Game strategy**
- **Estimation**
- **Chance**

Getting Ready

What You'll Need

Pattern Blocks, about half a shoebox-ful, per group

Dice, one die per group

Adding machine tape, or long strips of paper, 75 cm in length with starting and finishing lines marked 50 cm apart, one per child

Overhead Pattern Blocks (optional)

Overview

Children play a game in which they place Pattern Blocks along a strip of adding machine tape and attempt to wind up closest to the designated finish line. In this activity, children have the opportunity to:

- ◆ make estimates involving length
- ◆ develop strategic thinking skills

The Activity

When children play the game in *On Their Own*, you may want to have them place the tapes parallel to each other about 10 cm apart so they can compare the length of their paths as the game progresses.

Introducing

- ◆ Show children the race track made on a long strip of paper.
- ◆ Have a volunteer take a handful of Pattern Blocks and use them to form a path beginning at the starting line on the paper according to these rules:
  - There can be no space between the blocks.
  - The blocks may touch at their corners.
  - The blocks may touch along all or part of their sides.
  - The path must stay on the paper track.
- ◆ After the volunteer has finished, talk about other ways to use the same blocks to make a different path that follows the same rules. Arrange the paths next to one another and compare them.

©ETA/Cuisenaire®

On Their Own

Play *Closest to the Finish Line!*

Here are the rules:

1. This is a game for 3 or 4 players. The object of the game is to build a path of Pattern Blocks that ends closest to the finish line without going over it.

2. Each player gets a paper track that has a starting and finishing line marked.

3. Each player rolls a die and chooses that number of Pattern Blocks. The Pattern Blocks may be all the same or they may be a mixture of different kinds. Each player holds his or her blocks until everyone has rolled and picked their Pattern Blocks.

4. The players place the first block at the starting line. Then they place each of their other Pattern Blocks on their paper tracks so that each new block touches the last. All Pattern Blocks must be inside the paper.

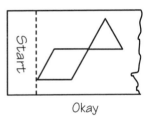
Okay

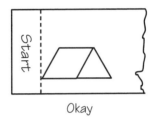
Okay

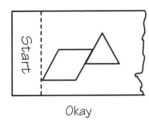
Okay

5. After everyone has rolled the die and placed Pattern Blocks on the path 5 times, the game is over.

6. The player to come closest to the finish line without going over it wins. If everyone goes over the finish line, the player who came closest to the finish line wins.

- Play several games of *Closest to the Finish Line*.

- Be ready to talk about the strategies you used to help you win the game.

The Bigger Picture

Thinking and Sharing

Invite volunteers to discuss the strategies they used while playing the game.

Use prompts like these to promote class discussion:

- ◆ Did you use the same strategy in every game? If so, what was it?

- ◆ Did your strategy change during the beginning, middle, or end of the game? Explain.

- ◆ Which blocks got you to the finish line fastest? slowest?

- ◆ How would you place these blocks if you wanted to cover a lot of distance? a little distance?

- ◆ Did the numbers of blocks you picked influence your strategy? How?

Drawing

Show a game that is "in progress" and has all but the last 6 to 8 cm of the tape filled with Pattern Block pieces. Have children draw a picture of what blocks they would choose if they rolled a 5 and how they would place them.

Teacher Talk

Where's the Mathematics?

This activity gives children an opportunity to work with estimations of non-standard measurement in a gamelike setting. The game requires strategy and some planning ahead to optimize the final plays. With only five rolls of the die, the game moves quickly so children have the opportunity to play it several times in a fairly short amount of time. This gives them ample time to test out several strategies and see which ones work best.

During the first game or two, children are learning the rules and their play tends to be somewhat random. After that, they begin to develop strategies that will help them win. Many of the strategies come from observing how their peers play the game and what seems to work—or not work—for them. At first they are apt to choose the blocks that are their favorite colors or shapes or "one of each." After a while, they begin to think in terms of estimating the distance left and considering how many rolls of the die remain.

This is a game in which the strategy changes as children get closer to the end of the game. Children will tell you that the first roll or two doesn't matter too much, but as their path gets closer to the finish line they need to more carefully consider which blocks to choose. If children still have a long way to go and only two or three rolls of the die left, they need to pick the larger blocks, for example the hexagon or trapezoid, and place the blocks so only the vertices (corners) touch. On the other hand, if they had rolled 5s and/or 6s on the first two rolls of the die and they are getting pretty close to the finish line, they have to choose smaller blocks and perhaps place the blocks so their sides touch. They need to consider what might happen if a 6 comes up on the final roll and ask themselves the question, "Will there be enough room left?" On the final roll, it can be quite a squeeze to fit in the required number of blocks if they are very close to the finish line.

     ©ETA/Cuisenaire®

Extending the Activity

Have children play the game with this change in the rules: After the first roll of the die, they must choose all of the same kind of Pattern Block. After their next roll of the die, they can select a different Pattern Block, but again must choose all of that kind of Pattern Block.

You will observe children placing one block against the other as they make their choices and try to minimize or maximize the distance covered by the blocks. To maximize the length, they will learn to use the longer diagonal of the tan parallelogram, the longer base of the trapezoid, or the diagonal of the hexagon.

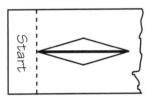 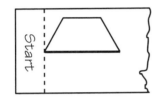 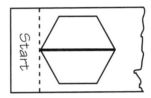

When trying to minimize the distance, their best choice is choosing triangles and creating a path that snakes around with the sides of the triangles touching.

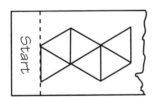

There's an element of chance in this game. Children can't control which number comes up next on the die. Occasionally, all of one kind of block has been used up before their turn and they have to make do with what remains in the shoebox of blocks. Having them pick their Pattern Blocks but keep them hidden in their hand until everyone has rolled the die also means that they can't let the choices of the other players influence what they are about to do.

COPY CAT

Getting Ready

What You'll Need

Pattern Blocks, about 30 per group

Paper, 12" x 18", 1 sheet per group

Ruler

Scissors

Overhead Pattern Blocks (optional)

Overview

Children use Pattern Blocks to create shapes that have reflective symmetry across a horizontal or vertical line. In this activity, children have the opportunity to:

◆ create a symmetrical shape, piece by piece

◆ decide whether or not a design has symmetry

The Activity

Working in threes in the On Their Own *activity ensures that children take turns at placing new blocks and then have a turn at balancing the symmetry of the design.*

Introducing

◆ Draw a thick vertical line down the center of a sheet of paper and display it. Place a Pattern Block so that one of its edges lies along this vertical line.

◆ Invite a volunteer to place another Pattern Block on the paper to make a design that is symmetrical about the line. Explain that the block must be placed on the other side of the line so that when you trace the blocks and fold the paper along the line, the two shapes will cover each other exactly.

◆ Trace around the two blocks, fold the paper along the line, and verify that the design is symmetrical.

◆ Unfold the paper and put the two blocks back as they were. Then invite another volunteer to place a block on one side of the line of symmetry so it is touching at least one of the blocks already placed there. Then call on a third volunteer to place a block on the other side to "balance" that block and keep the design symmetrical.

◆ Continue having volunteers add blocks to the design, and balance it to keep it symmetrical.

On Their Own

Can you make a design that can fold over itself exactly?

- Work in groups of 3. Together decide whether you want a horizontal or a vertical line of symmetry. Fold your paper in half to make that line of symmetry.

  Horizontal line   Vertical line

- Open the paper back up and use a ruler to draw a heavy line over the fold mark.
- Now work together to make a big shape that is exactly the same on both sides of the line. Here's how:
  - Take turns placing Pattern Blocks.
  - The person who goes first must place a block so one of its edges touches the line of symmetry without crossing it.
  - The next person places the same kind block on the other side of the line so that the new design is symmetrical.
  - The third person adds a different block so that one of its edges touches at least one of the blocks already placed on the design.
  - The person who went first "balances" this new block so the whole design is symmetrical.
  - Keep taking turns building your design until everyone decides that it is a symmetrical design you all like.
- Trace around the outside of all of the blocks.
- Carefully slide the paper out from underneath the blocks, trying to leave your design in place.
- Cut out your shape and fold it along the line to see if the 2 parts cover each other exactly.
- Make another design using a different line of symmetry.

The Bigger Picture

Thinking and Sharing

Have each group select their favorite symmetrical design. Help children to post them. Invite each group to explain how they went about making their design.

Use prompts such as these to promote class discussion:

- Which was easier to work with, the horizontal or vertical line of symmetry? Why?
- Were some blocks harder to place than others? Explain.
- Which job did you like better, placing the block or "balancing" the design? Why?
- How does folding help to show that the two parts of a shape are exactly the same?
- Did you have any other way of knowing if the parts matched? If so, tell how.
- Does your design have another line of symmetry? How can you tell?

Extending the Activity

1. After children have completed placing all the blocks in their symmetrical design, have them take turns removing any block from one side of the design and then its reflected block from the other side of the design. Children should keep taking turns removing blocks until no more blocks remain.

Teacher Talk

Where's the Mathematics?

This activity gives children a chance to use reflective symmetry creatively. By building their symmetrical designs one block at a time, children become deeply involved in noticing how each component contributes to the symmetrical outcome of the design. Children are likely to report that the vertical line of symmetry was slightly easier to work with than the horizontal line. This may be due to the fact that objects with a vertical line of symmetry—for example, people, buildings, and trees—are more abundant in the environment than are those with horizontal lines of symmetry. Thus, children are already familiar with symmetry with respect to vertical lines on an intuitive level. (Where children sit in relation to the line of symmetry may, of course, turn a horizontal line into a vertical line, and vice versa.)

This activity is deceptively easy at the start, but becomes more complicated as a design grows. Different children cite different blocks as "the block most difficult to work with." For some, the number of sides on the hexagon seems to be confusing: It isn't clear which of the sides the "balancing" piece should be placed against. The shift in direction caused by some of the angles on the other shapes may give children pause as they have to reassess how the other side of the design needs to change in response to the directional shift caused by placing one of these kinds of blocks on one side of the shape.

A few designs may have more than one line of symmetry, especially early on in the process of building the design. These multiple lines of symmetry may have occurred if children limited their choice of Pattern Blocks to the ones

2. Change the rules so children place two blocks on one side of the design on each of their turns.

---

that have multiple lines of symmetry, that is, triangles, squares, both parallelograms, and hexagons.

As designs become more complicated, these multiple lines of symmetry may well disappear.

Some children may think their designs have reflective symmetry when, in fact, they do not. The picture on the left shows reflective symmetry, since the design can be folded along the axis of symmetry and the two sides will coincide. Although the picture on the right has rotational symmetry, it does not have reflective symmetry because it does not pass the fold test.

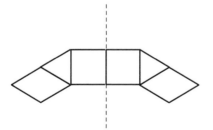 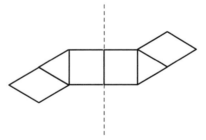

COVER THE CATERPILLAR

- Counting
- Equivalence
- Patterns

Getting Ready

What You'll Need

Pattern Blocks, at least 6 yellow, 20 blue, and 40 green per pair

Cover the Caterpillar outlines, page 90

Crayons

Overview

Children find combinations of blue and green Pattern Blocks that can be used to cover four yellow hexagons. In this activity, children have the opportunity to:

- ◆ use patterns to solve a problem
- ◆ work with equivalence in a geometric context

The Activity

Introducing

- ◆ Ask children to find a way to cover their yellow Pattern Block using exactly 4 blocks.
- ◆ Confirm that the only combination that works is 2 blue blocks and 2 green blocks. Record this finding on the board:

Number of Blue	Number of Green	Total Number
2	2	4

- ◆ Now ask children to cover the hexagon using exactly 5 blocks.
- ◆ Again, elicit that there is only one solution: 1 blue block and 4 green blocks. Add this information to the chart.

Number of Blue	Number of Green	Total Number
2	2	4
1	4	5

On Their Own

> *How many different ways can you use only blue and green Pattern Blocks to cover the caterpillar?*
>
> - Work with a partner.
>
> - Put 4 yellow blocks together to make your caterpillar so it looks like this:
>
>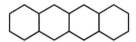
>
> - Use only blue and green Pattern Blocks to cover your caterpillar.
>
> - Record your solution by coloring the caterpillar outline.
>
> - Keep track of the number of blue blocks you used and the number of green blocks you used. Also keep track of the total number of blocks you used.
>
> - Now use different numbers of blue and green blocks to cover the caterpillar. Record these results.
>
> - Repeat the activity several times.
>
> - Look for patterns in your work.

The Bigger Picture

Thinking and Sharing

Invite children to discuss how they worked on the activity. Then have them help you create a class chart with the headings *Number of Blue Blocks*, *Number of Green Blocks*, and *Total Number of Blocks*. Patterns may be easier for children to see if you arrange their data in order by the total number of blocks used.

Illustrate data in the chart with children's colored-in caterpillars.

Use prompts such as these to promote class discussion:

- How many different combinations of blue and green blocks did you find that will cover the caterpillar?

- What is the greatest number of blocks that anyone used? What is the least?

- What strategies did you use for solving this problem?

- Did you change strategies as you worked? If so, how did you change, and why?

- Did you notice any patterns that helped you find solutions? Is so, describe them.

- Do you think our class chart includes all of the solutions? If not, which ones do you think might be missing?

Extending the Activity

1. Ask children to repeat the activity for a caterpillar made of six hexagons and compare the results with those for the four-hexagon caterpillar.

Teacher Talk

Where's the Mathematics?

There are a variety of ways in which children investigate this problem. Some may use trial and error. Others may begin by trial and error and then develop a systematic approach. No matter what strategies they choose, children find that there are many different combinations of blue and green blocks that can be used to cover the caterpillar, and that they must do lots of counting.

Children may begin their search for solutions by covering the hexagons using only blue parallelograms. This will require 12 blocks, the smallest number of total blocks needed. They may then find additional solutions by substituting two green triangles for each blue parallelogram. Other children may begin the other way by covering the hexagons entirely with green triangles. They may realize that this arrangement will utilize the largest number of blocks (24). They may then substitute one of the blue parallelograms for two green triangles to make a new solution. After children have used this substitution strategy several times, they may be able to fill in the chart without actually working with the blocks because they have found a pattern. This chart shows the 13 solutions:

Blue	Green	Total
0	24	24
1	22	23
2	20	22
3	18	21
4	16	20
5	14	19
6	12	18
7	10	17
8	8	16
9	6	15
10	4	14
11	2	13
12	0	12

2. Present other problems in which children must cover a particular set of blocks with a specified number of other blocks of two or three colors.

When children are asked to describe the patterns they notice, they are apt to point out that as the numbers in the blue column increase by one, the numbers in the green column decrease by two. This describes what was happening when they traded in two triangles for one parallelogram. They may also notice that the numbers in the total column decrease by one. This happens because every time they trade in two triangles for one parallelogram, they have one less piece left on the caterpillar. Others may note that the number of green blocks is always an even number and that the number of blue blocks could be either even or odd.

If the class has not discovered all the solutions and there are "holes" in the chart, they may be able to predict what solutions are missing and then use the Pattern Blocks to verify them. When the patterns appear to be complete, it is likely that the chart contains all of the possible solutions.

As they search for patterns and organize the data into a chart, children come to see how these strategies can be useful in solving problems. Helping children to relate the changes in the numbers back to what they were doing with the Pattern Blocks in the activity enables them to recognize the connection between their work and the resulting mathematics.

HOW MANY SEATS?

NUMBER • GEOMETRY • PATTERNS/FUNCTIONS

- Spatial visualization
- Multiples
- Counting

Getting Ready

What You'll Need

Pattern Blocks, 13 squares and 13 trapezoids per pair

Overhead Pattern Blocks (optional)

Overview

Children use Pattern Blocks to model a problem involving the number of tables needed to seat a given number of guests. In this activity, children have an opportunity to:

- ◆ solve an open-ended problem
- ◆ explore concepts of multiplication, division, and remainders
- ◆ explore patterns that allow them to count more efficiently

The Activity

Introducing

- ◆ On the chalkboard, draw a square and a trapezoid.
- ◆ Ask children to pretend that each of these blocks is a table: The orange square seats four people and the red trapezoid seats five.
- ◆ Invite volunteers to come up and draw a picture that shows how many people could be seated if two square tables were used. Their drawings are likely to look something like this:
- ◆ Invite children to do the same thing for two trapezoids. Make sure drawings show that if the long sides of the trapezoids are put together, the answer is 6 seats; if short sides are put together, the answer is 8 seats.

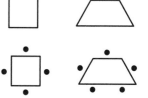

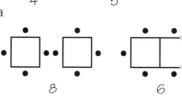

©ETA/Cuisenaire®

On Their Own

Imagine that you are in charge of arranging the tables for a school lunch party. How could you set up the tables so there are enough seats for everyone?

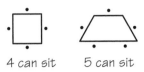

4 can sit   5 can sit

- Work with a partner. Pretend that the orange and the red Pattern Blocks are tables. Arrange the 2 kinds of tables to seat 25 people. You can use separate tables or put tables together to make larger tables.

- Try to come up with a few different arrangements that work.

- Record each solution.

- Choose the arrangement that you think works best. Be ready to tell the class why you picked it.

The Bigger Picture

Thinking and Sharing

Invite each pair of children to come to the chalkboard, show one of their solutions, and explain how it works. Continue until children have no more solutions.

Use prompts like these to promote class discussion:

- How did you count the number of seats? Did you do it one-by-one or did you have a quicker method?

- Did you notice any patterns when you were counting?

- Why did you think one of your solutions was the best?

- Which solutions have the exact number of seats that are needed? Which have extra seats?

- Which solution uses the fewest tables? How was that solution possible?

- Which solution uses the greatest number of tables? How was that solution possible?

- Do you need more tables if you keep the tables separate or if you put them together? Why?

- If your class wanted to have one big table, which arrangement would use the fewest tables?

Drawing

Have children draw a picture for the school custodian that explains how to set up the tables for the lunch on which the activity is based.

Teacher Talk

Where's the Mathematics?

This is an open-ended problem of the kind people are likely to face in life when planning for a large function. In addition to satisfying the need for 25 seats, people also consider factors such as whether to have one large table or several smaller tables and whether to use only one shape of table or combine different types.

If children choose to place the tables separately, they may use a counting pattern that incorporates the multiples 2, 4, or 5. Two of the solutions, shown below, lead to exactly 25 seats. The first uses six tables and the second uses five.

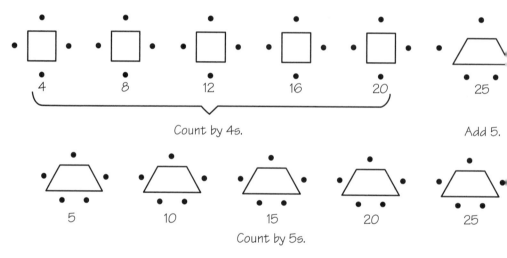

Count by 4s.   Add 5.

Count by 5s.

There are several more solutions using separate tables, but each of these has seats leftover. Although children are unlikely to present these solutions in chart form, the following chart makes a quick reference for you. The solutions shown keep the seating as close to 25 as possible.

No. of trapezoids	No. of squares	No. of seats	No. of leftover seats
0	7	28	3
2	4	26	1
3	3	27	2
4	2	28	3

When children are asked to select one solution as the "best," and to defend their answer, they are apt to present many reasons for selecting a solution. Children may select the solutions pictured above because these arrangements seat exactly 25. Furthermore, they may select the trapezoidal table solution because it uses the fewest tables.

Extending the Activity

1. Have children show how they would arrange square tables and trapezoid tables if each child in the problem invited one family member to come to lunch.

2. Ask children to work in groups to consider what other shapes (not necessarily Pattern Block shapes) would work well for this problem.

Children may prefer any one of the solutions presented in the chart because they have leftover seats which allow people more room to spread out. On the other hand, the solution using seven square tables may be more aesthetically pleasing to them since it repeats the same shape.

Some children may choose to build one large table, and either use all tables of the same shape, or mix the shapes, as shown below:

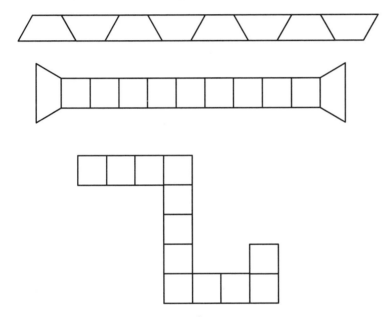

Once again, you are likely to see the children count by twos, or even threes, as they find the total number of seats. Children discover that this type of solution uses more tables, because when two tables are pushed together, one or two sides of each table is lost.

No matter how they arrange the tables, children must do a lot of counting, and are likely to recognize that the numbers seem to occur in regular patterns.

This activity can also provide an informal introduction to the concepts of *division* and *remainders*. For example, children who find that 25 seats can be divided equally into five equal groups of five may come to realize that they are modeling the division 25 ÷ 5. Similarly, children who provide solutions that include extra seats may be able to see the extra seats as representing a remainder.

LOOK HOW I'M GROWING

Getting Ready

What You'll Need

Pattern Blocks, about 20-25 per pair
Crayons
Overhead Pattern Blocks (optional)

Overview

Children build the first two stages of a pattern using Pattern Blocks. Then other children extend the pattern and describe how the shape is growing. In this activity, children have the opportunity to:

◆ create and identify growing patterns

◆ use patterns to make predictions

◆ describe the patterns they see

The Activity

Introducing

◆ Display this Pattern Block design. Explain that this design is your beginning design and that you are going to add blocks to make the design grow.

◆ Create the next stage of the design as children watch.

◆ Call on volunteers to explain how your *beginning design* and your *growing design* are alike and different.

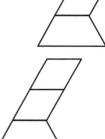

◆ Ask children to use their Pattern Blocks to create the next stage of growth of the design. When they have finished, invite them to share this third stage of the design, or *"grown-up design."*

On Their Own

Can you create a growing design and challenge your partner to make it grow again?

- Work with a partner.

- One partner uses Pattern Blocks to create a design. Then that partner builds the design again and adds one or more blocks to any part of the design to make it grow. For example:

Beginning design   Growing design

- The other partner tries to continue the same growing pattern by adding one or more blocks to the Growing design to make a Grown-Up design. This partner should also describe how the pattern grows.

Grown-up design

- Both partners trace the three designs and color the blocks used.

- Now switch roles and repeat the activity.

The Bigger Picture

Thinking and Sharing

Invite volunteers to display the three designs of one of their favorite growth patterns. Children can use Pattern Blocks to predict what they think the fourth design (a more grown-up design) would be. The partners who are displaying the original three designs can then circulate and look for the fourth design they had in mind. Repeat this process with a few other children's three-stage designs. You may also wish to have children illustrate their work with blocks on the overhead.

Use prompts like these to promote class discussion:

- ◆ What part of this design was growing? How was it growing?

- ◆ Look at the *beginning design* and the *growing design* of this pattern. Can anyone think of a different *grown-up design*? What is it?

- ◆ What would the fourth and fifth stages of growth look like?

- ◆ Which was harder—making the first two designs or predicting the third design? Why?

- ◆ Did any of the designs have similar growth patterns? Which ones?

Extending the Activity

1. Have children build patterns as they did in the lesson, but this time predict the number of blocks used in each other's next design. Encourage children to record the number of blocks used in each of the three stages and then extend that number pattern as far as they can.

Teacher Talk

Where's the Mathematics?

Activities such as this help children to look for patterns and to learn to use these patterns to make predictions. Some children can see patterns more easily in the block designs than in the numbers generated by these designs. For other children, the reverse may be true. The aim should be to have children recognize patterns and use them to make predictions about what comes next.

Many children will be able to build the next stage in the pattern but they will not be able to verbalize why they are building it that way. Hearing other children's explanations of how patterns are growing will help these children learn how to articulate what is going on in their heads. For example, a child might look at this pattern and say that, "You keep counting up...2,3,4."

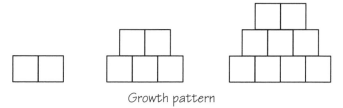

Growth pattern

Another child might verbalize the pattern as "adding another row that has one more in it." Their explanations may be sketchy and you may want to ask for clarification. Their ability to put a pattern into words will be a valuable skill in mathematics, especially in algebra.

If any children are unable to see a pattern in other children's designs, the children involved might talk about the designs. In some cases, children may come up with designs that don't grow predictably, and you may have to intervene to help children to see the problem in their design and get them started on something that works.

Initially, some children may not understand that a growth pattern means that the design is getting larger. Children may predict that the third stage will be a repetition of the first stage because they confuse earlier work done with "ababab" patterns with growth patterns. It may help to ask them to build the second stage, or "Growing Design," and then add on to it.

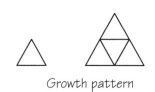

Growth pattern

2. Show children the first two stages of a pattern that is "shrinking" because blocks are removed in a predictable way. Ask children to continue and describe the shrinking pattern.

Some children may make growth patterns that have more than one possible answer for the third stage, or "Grown-up Design." For example, in the pattern below, the third stage could either have three squares in the bottom step and follow the pattern 1, 2, 3, 4,... or it could have 4 squares in the bottom layer and follow the pattern that each new step is a double of the last step, or 1, 2, 4, 8, ...

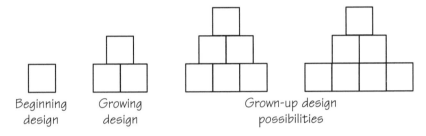

Beginning   Growing   Grown-up design
design   design   possibilities

When asked if any of the designs have similar growth patterns, some children may be so focused on the visual patterns that they will answer "no" because none of the patterns looked identical. Other children may answer "yes" because they have looked at the underlying counting patterns that are the same. These children are demonstrating an ability to generalize when they look at these two patterns. They will say that the patterns below are similar because the first kept adding one more triangle and the second kept adding one more square; or, even though the shapes—triangles and squares—were different, the counting pattern was the same.

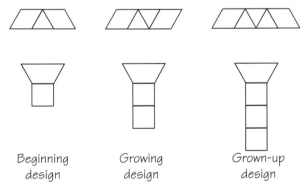

Beginning   Growing   Grown-up
design   design   design

Encourage this recognition of the generalization of patterning because good problem solvers are those children who have learned to see what seemingly unrelated problems can have in common. Many of the growth patterns that children design will grow by using the counting numbers so there should be many examples of common growth patterns for children to recognize.

ONE HUNDRED

- **Estimating**
- **Comparing**
- **Area**
- **Counting**
- **Spatial reasoning**

Getting Ready

What You'll Need

Pattern Blocks, 100 of the same shape per group

Pattern Block triangle paper, page 91

Poster paper, 5 sheets per group

Crayons

Overhead Pattern Blocks (optional)

Overview

Children estimate the area that would be covered by a given number of Pattern Blocks. In this activity, children have the opportunity to:

- ◆ make and adjust estimates
- ◆ compare area

The Activity

Introducing

- ◆ Display a yellow hexagon and a piece of paper. Have children estimate how much of the paper ten yellow blocks would cover.
- ◆ Ask a volunteer to show his or her estimate by drawing on the paper a shape into which the ten yellow blocks would just fit. At the same time, have the rest of the class draw their own shapes to show their estimates.
- ◆ Check the volunteer's estimate by placing ten hexagons on the shape that the he or she drew. Have the rest of the class do the same on their own shapes. Point out that the yellow blocks should be placed so that there is no space between them, as shown.

- ◆ Ask children whether their estimates are larger than, smaller than, or about the same as the area actually covered by the blocks.

©ETA/Cuisenaire®

On Their Own

How much poster paper will 100 Pattern Blocks cover?

- Start with 10 Pattern Blocks of the same kind. Decide with your group which kind of block to use.

- Working with a partner, put the 10 blocks together on a piece of poster paper. Make sure no paper shows between them.

- Now use the 10 blocks to estimate how much paper 100 blocks will cover. Use crayons, triangle paper, and scissors to help you make your estimate.

- Next, meet with your group to share estimates.

- Decide on one group estimate, and draw it on poster paper.

- Count out 100 blocks of the same kind. (Share this job with your group members.) Place 50 of the blocks on top of your estimate. Don't leave any spaces between the blocks.

- Discuss whether you want to change your estimate.

- If you make a new estimate, draw it next to the old estimate on the poster paper.

- Put the rest of the blocks on the poster paper, leaving no spaces. Trace around the big shape that the 100 blocks make. Remove the blocks and color in your shape to match the blocks.

- Be ready to talk about whether your estimate was too big, too small, or about right.

The Bigger Picture

Thinking and Sharing

Have volunteers display their results for each kind of block.

Use prompts such as these to promote class discussion:

- Which group of 100 blocks covered the greatest area? Why?
- How did you make your first estimate about how much area 100 blocks would cover?
- Did you change your estimate? If so, why?
- Was your final estimate too large, too small, or about right?

Extending the Activity

1. Have groups of children use 10 blocks and a ruler to estimate how long a wall of 100 blocks would stretch.

2. Have groups estimate how many blocks of a different color would fit in

Where's the Mathematics?

This activity can help children to realize that an estimate is not merely a guess. An estimate depends on having a benchmark, or reference point, that can serve as a standard for comparing or judging things. Children are encouraged to first use ten Pattern Blocks to make a benchmark for themselves. Children approach this problem in a variety of ways. Some children may use nonstandard measurement and group the ten blocks so the configuration has roughly the same shape as something already familiar to them—for example, a handprint or a postcard. Children may then, either physically or mentally, move their configuration around on the paper until an estimate is reached.

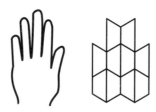

Other children might make a row of the ten blocks, then mentally duplicate that row again and again until they think they have reached 100.

Children with a well-developed sense about the number 100 may already know that 100 can be thought of as 10 groups of 10. These children might place their 10 blocks in a horizontal row, draw that line, then move the blocks in a vertical row, draw that line, and use those two dimensions to envision the 100 blocks as 10 rows of 10 blocks.

By being allowed to revise their estimates after placing 50 of the blocks into their drawings, children are creating a new benchmark using half of the number of blocks they will need. They are also learning to think critically and to recognize that sometimes it may be necessary to revise an answer when presented with additional data.

the shapes they drew in *On Their Own*. For example, if a group created a shape that was an estimate for 100 red blocks, they can now estimate how many green blocks would cover the same shape.

Children may use a variety of counting strategies when counting out 100 of their designated blocks. They may count by twos, fives, tens, or by any other number that they are comfortable using. Counting out 100 blocks may be a chore for young children. Fortunately, group members can act as checks on the accuracy of each member's counting.

When groups compare their results with those of their classmates, ideas about area may emerge. For example, if two or more groups used the same kind of Pattern Block, they may be surprised to see how different their 100-block shapes look. The shapes below were each made from 100 green triangles.

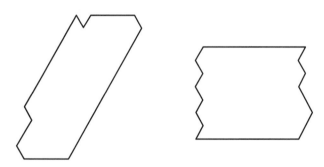

Children may also notice that the relative sizes of the 100-block shapes made from different Pattern Blocks are the same as the relative sizes of the individual blocks. For example, a shape made from 100 yellow hexagons will be twice as large as a shape made from 100 red trapezoids, since a yellow hexagon is twice as large as a red trapezoid. If no group chose a particular Pattern Block shape, children can compare the area of one of those blocks to that of a block they did use, and use the size relationship to predict how much area 100 blocks of the new shape will cover. Through this use of the blocks, children strengthen their understanding of area and relative measurement.

PATTERN BLOCK PIZZA

- Counting
- Equivalence
- Chance
- Area
- Fractions

Getting Ready

What You'll Need

Pattern Blocks, about 14 trapezoids, 25 blue parallelograms, and 40 green triangles per pair

Pattern Block Pizza game board, page 92

Pattern Block Pizza Topping spinner, page 93

Crayons

Overhead Pattern Blocks (optional)

Overview

In this game for two players, children take turns trying to cover hexagon "pizzas" with Pattern Block "toppings." In this activity, children have the opportunity to:

- ◆ develop the concept of equivalence

- ◆ develop an intuitive understanding of probability

- ◆ work informally with halves, thirds, and sixths

The Activity

Introducing

- ◆ Ask children to imagine that they are going to a pizzeria in Pattern Block Town where all the pizzas are the same size and shape as the yellow block and the toppings are represented by the red, blue, and green Pattern Blocks.

- ◆ Ask children for ideas on what kinds of toppings the red, blue, and green blocks could stand for.

- ◆ Call on a volunteer to be a pizza maker and to cover a pizza completely with toppings.

- ◆ Call on another volunteer to show another way to cover a pizza completely.

- ◆ Then play part of a game of *Pattern Block Pizza* with the children before they begin the *On Their Own*.

On Their Own

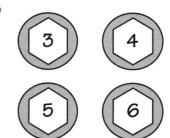

Play Pattern Block Pizza!

Here are the rules.

1. This is a game for 2 players. The object of the game is to completely cover 6 pizzas with toppings. In this game, the pizzas are the size and shape of yellow Pattern Blocks, and the toppings are the red, blue, and green blocks.

2. Each player needs a Pizza game board showing pizzas numbered 1 through 6.

3. The first player spins the Pizza Topping spinner. Whatever topping comes up, the player puts that Pattern Block shape on Pizza 1 on the game board.

4. Then the second player spins the spinner and puts a block on Pizza 1 on his or her game board.

5. Each player must completely fill one pizza before moving on to the next pizza.

6. If a player gets a Pattern Block that is too large to fit on the pizza, he or she can exchange that Pattern Block for smaller ones that add up to the shape spun.

7. Players keep taking turns until both players have 6 full pizzas.

- When you have finished playing the game, trace around the toppings on the game board and color them in.

- If you have time, play the game again.

The Bigger Picture

Thinking and Sharing

Ask for volunteers to bring up completed game boards for display. Invite children to talk about their game and describe some of the thinking they did.

Use prompts such as these to promote class discussion.

- ◆ How do the posted game boards differ?
- ◆ Did anyone find another way to cover a pizza? Show us.
- ◆ How many different ways can a pizza be covered?
- ◆ Are there any ways to cover a pizza that never came up? Why do you think they never came up?
- ◆ Did you ever trade a block for others? When did you do this?
- ◆ What kinds of trades could you make?

Drawing

Have children draw covered Pattern Block pizzas that form designs they like.

Extending the Activity

1. Make a tally of how often each of the six pizza combinations came up. Ask children to explain why certain combinations showed up more often or less often than others.

Teacher Talk

Where's the Mathematics?

This activity provides children with an informal look at fractions. The symbolic language of fractions does not need to be introduced; the approach can be very low-key by keeping the focus on the geometric shapes and referring to the blocks by color rather than geometric name. Nevertheless, as children put the toppings on their pizzas, they are learning all the ways in which one whole (the yellow hexagon) can be formed using halves (the red trapezoids), thirds (the blue parallelograms), and sixths (the green triangles). There are seven possible combinations for covering the pizzas:

Some children may initially think that a pizza is "different" if it has the same toppings arranged in a different way. Here is an example of two pizzas that have the same toppings arranged differently.

2. Have children play the game again with this change: When they spin a topping that is too large to fit on their pizza, they must give their opponent the chance to use it.

3. Have children design a new spinner with different number of sectors and/or different choices of toppings. Have them play the game with the new spinner and compare results with the *On Their Own*.

Theoretically, the posted class results should show that green triangles were used most often as toppings—even if children made very few or no exchanges of blocks in the course of the game. Some children may be able to make the connection that there are more green triangles because there are more sectors on the spinner for the triangle. This kind of observation lays the foundation for understanding probability and how games of chance work.

As children trade larger blocks for smaller ones they are being informally introduced to equivalent fractions. For example, a trapezoid (1/2) may be traded for a parallelogram (1/3) and a triangle (1/6) or for three triangles (3/6). When making these trades, children may not see the trapezoid as 1/2 of the original hexagon. They may instead see it as a new whole and therefore define the triangle as 1/3 of the trapezoid and the parallelogram as 2/3 of the trapezoid. Hence, the triangle could be thought of as 1/6 of the hexagon or 1/3 of the trapezoid or 1/2 of the parallelogram. Learning that a fraction is defined in terms of how large the whole is is an important lesson that many children struggle with. Having these concrete experiences with Pattern Blocks can help to lay the foundation for understanding the concept of fractions.

This lesson on fractions is nicely connected to the geometric concept of area. The equivalent trades may be made because the pieces have equivalent areas. For example, a parallelogram and a triangle fit exactly on top of a trapezoid.

Children's experience in playing the game of Pattern Block Pizza may provide them with an intuitive basis for future work with area, fractions, and probability.

PATTERN BLOCK TOY FACTORY

NUMBER • GEOMETRY

- Counting
- Comparing
- Money
- Addition
- Multiplication

Getting Ready

What You'll Need

Pattern Blocks, 10-12 red, blue, yellow, and green per child

Toy Catalog, page 94

Counters or play money (optional)

Crayons

Overview

Children use Pattern Blocks to design toys. Given the monetary value of the green triangle, red trapezoid, blue parallelogram, and yellow hexagon, children then find the total cost of their designs. In this activity, children have the opportunity to:

- ◆ compare and combine numerical quantities
- ◆ work with money concepts
- ◆ use proportional thinking
- ◆ recognize the size relationships among different geometric shapes

The Activity

In On Their Own, prices could be scaled up for older children.

Introducing

- ◆ Arrange and display a blue parallelogram and two green triangles, as shown. Ask children to pretend that this is a Pattern Block design for a toy. Invite them to say what the toy could be.

- ◆ Ask children to suppose that when you buy a toy, its price is based only on its size. Have children discuss how much this Pattern Block toy might cost if one triangle costs 1¢.

- ◆ Establish that each triangle would be 1¢ and the blue parallelogram would cost 2¢ because it is twice the size of the triangle. Therefore, the toy would cost 4¢.

- ◆ Invite volunteers to explain how, if a green triangle costs 1¢, they would price this design for a clown's hat.

- ◆ Establish that since the triangle is worth 1¢ and the trapezoid holds three green triangles, the trapezoid will cost 3¢ and the clown's hat will cost 4¢.

On Their Own

Pretend you are designing a Pattern Block toy for a toy company's catalog. if you know how much each kind of a block costs, can you figure out the cost of the toy?

- Work with a partner. Each of you use 3 to 6 Pattern Blocks to create a new toy that will be shown in the toy factory's catalog. Make sure the blocks lie flat.

- Each of you trace the shape of your toy on your Toy Catalog page. Then color in the separate blocks.

- Write down the name of your toy.

- Now use the price on the bottom of the Toy Catalog page to help you to find out how much your toy costs. Write down that price.

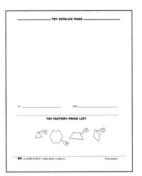

The Bigger Picture

Thinking and Sharing

Ask for volunteers to share their Toy Catalog pages with the class. Post these worksheets so that everyone can see them. Ask the volunteers to tell how much each toy picture is worth.

Use prompts like these to promote class discussion:

- What strategy did you use to find the cost of the toy?
- Could anyone else use a different strategy to find the cost of the same toy?
- Which toy is the most expensive? Why do you think so?
- Which toy is the least expensive? Why do you think so?

Writing

Have children explain how, if they knew the price of the green triangle, they would be able to find the cost of any toy design that used green triangles, blue parallelograms, red trapezoids, and yellow hexagons.

Extending the Activity

1. Have the children make a graph of their designs, grouping them by cost, type of toy, or any attribute they find interesting.

2. Have children sort the designs by those less than 5¢, those exactly 5¢, and those worth more than 5¢. What conclusions can children draw?

Teacher Talk

Where's the Mathematics?

Listening to the strategies that children use to figure the total cost of their toys gives you an opportunity to assess the sophistication of their computation skills. For example, children may approach this problem of finding the cost of this "toy" in several ways:

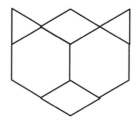

One child might simply add up the prices shape by shape: 2¢ + 12¢ + 4¢ + 4¢ + 12¢ + 2¢ = 36¢. Another may group the shapes into pairs of triangles (4¢) plus pairs of parallelograms (8¢) plus pairs of hexagons (24¢), and then add these prices for a total of 36¢. A third child might physically or mentally convert some or all of the shapes to triangles and see 18 triangles at 2¢ each for a total of 36¢. Yet another child might see that the triangle-hexagon-parallelogram pattern has been repeated and double the 18¢ to get 36¢.

Using the question, "Could anyone else use a different strategy to find the cost of this same toy?" challenges children to focus on the problem-solving strategy rather than the answer. Children are helped to develop better mental math skills when they can see that there are many approaches to solving a problem.

3. Let children investigate both the fewest and the greatest number of Pattern Blocks needed to make a design worth exactly 8¢.

4. Ask children to change the value of the green triangle, then find the values of the other three blocks and the value of their toys.

If you decide to do the lesson extension in which children change the price of the Pattern Blocks, making up tables to compare how the prices have changed can contribute to the idea of proportional thinking—especially for older children. For example, the first column below shows the values when the original cost was 2¢ for a triangle. The second column shows that if the cost of the triangle were doubled, all of the values double. The third column could either be compared to the original column, in which case, everything has increased by a factor of 4, or it could be compared to the second column, in which case, everything has doubled. Children can establish new costs and make predictions about the values that will fill the rest of the chart, then verify their predictions with the Pattern Blocks.

	orig. cost	new cost	new cost
triangle	2¢	4¢	8¢
parallelogram	4	8	16
trapezoid	6	12	24
hexagon	12	24	48
my toy	?	?	?

That two different designs can have the same value (area) but look different is an important mathematical concept. While finding the value of various toys, children can notice that some have the same value, but will not readily observe that they have the same area, especially if the toys were composed of different Pattern Blocks. Some children, however, may conclude that the toys with greatest value also have the greatest area.

PATTERN BLOCK WALLS

- Counting
- Pattern recognition
- Using patterns

Getting Ready

What You'll Need

Pattern Blocks, (no orange or tan), about 20 of each shape per pair

Strips of paper, about 2½" x 30", 1 per pair

Overhead Pattern Blocks (optional)

Overview

Children identify patterns, then choose one pattern to repeat in a Pattern Block wall. They then determine how many blocks would be needed to extend this patterned wall. In this activity, children have the opportunity to:

- ◆ count
- ◆ recognize patterns
- ◆ use patterns to make predictions

The Activity

Introducing

- ◆ Display a Pattern Block wall like the one below. Have children use Pattern Blocks to copy the wall.

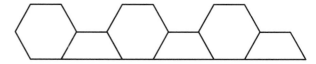

- ◆ Ask children how many different kinds of blocks they used to build their wall, and how many blocks they used altogether.

- ◆ Help children to realize that the first kind of block is followed by the second kind of block, and this same design is repeated twice more. Confirm that the basic pattern of the wall is made up of two different blocks that repeat.

- ◆ Ask a volunteer to show the next two blocks in the pattern while children do so at their seats.

©ETA/Cuisenaire®

On Their Own

Can you figure out what Pattern Blocks you will need to make a wall with a pattern that repeats 10 times?

- Look at the 5 pictures below. In each picture, a set of Pattern Blocks is repeated twice. Decide what the pattern is in each picture.

- Work with a partner. Chose the pattern in one of the pictures to use in a Pattern Block wall. Use Pattern Blocks to copy what you see. Make your wall stand like a real wall.

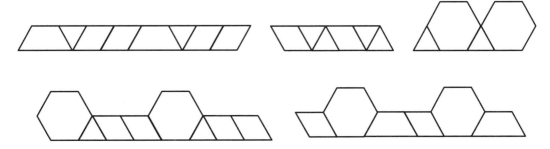

- Continue building your wall, repeating the pattern 5 times.

- Trace your work on a paper strip and color it in. Count and write down how many blocks of each kind you used, and how many blocks you used altogether.

- Try to think of way to know how many blocks of each kind and how many total blocks you will need to make the wall pattern repeat a total of 10 times.

- Now complete the wall and count the blocks to check whether your numbers were close.

- Be ready to talk about what you did and what you found out.

The Bigger Picture

Thinking and Sharing

Create columns by displaying each of the five patterns across the chalkboard. Then have pairs post their drawings in the appropriate column.

Use prompts like these to promote class discussion:

- Which wall or walls took the fewest blocks to build? How many blocks did you need? How many of each color block did you need?

- Which wall or walls took the most blocks to build? How many blocks did you need? How many of each color block did you need?

- What are some ways to know what blocks you will need for a wall pattern before you build the entire wall?

Extending the Activity

Have children work with their partners, taking turns creating patterns and extending each other's patterns.

Where's the Mathematics?

The colors, relative sizes, and design of Pattern Blocks allow certain shapes to fit together smoothly, and make building walls a self-correcting activity. As children identify patterns and create walls involving a given number of repetitions of a pattern, they are informally introduced to the concept that each pattern has a *core*—the name given to the original set of blocks that becomes repeated. Some children may struggle to identify the core. For these children, it may help for you to augment the visual pattern by reciting the colors involved; for example, "yellow, blue, green, yellow, blue, green," and so forth. By so doing, you can engage children's auditory sense so that it tunes in to the rhythm that is involved in the pattern. This, in turn, may enable children to identify the original core.

Children may use the structure of various patterns to help them calculate the total numbers of blocks and the number of blocks of each color needed for their wall. While some children, especially the younger ones, may be unable to find this information without constructing the entire wall and counting, others may use strategies such as doubling, skip counting, or multiplication. For example, a child might skip count to find the number of triangles in the wall shown on the following page, saying that "each repetition requires two triangles, so ten repetitions require 2, 4, 6, 8, 10, 12, 14, 16, 18, 20 green blocks altogether." He or she may further notice that each repetition also has one blue parallelogram, so 10 blue parallelograms are required for the whole wall. The total number of blocks needed, therefore, is 20 + 10, or 30.

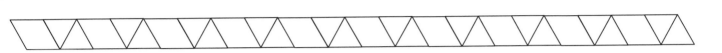

Since there are three blocks in the core, and there needs to be ten repetitions, multiplying 3 x 10 also gives the total number of blocks needed.

As children discuss which walls take the most blocks to build, they may be able to generalize that the greater the number of blocks there are in the original core, the greater the number of blocks there will be in the completed wall. A wall that has only two blocks in its core will require 20 blocks for the whole wall, whereas a wall with four blocks in its core will require twice as many, or 40 blocks, to complete 10 repetitions. The use of 10 repetitions for a whole wall will introduce many opportunities for children to practice using the multiples of 10 in their work and their discussions.

RED, GREEN, OR YELLOW?

- • Counting
- • Volume
- • Estimation
- • Predicting

Getting Ready

What You'll Need

Pattern Blocks, green triangles, red trapezoids, and yellow hexagons, sorted, 1/2 the amount needed to fill the big container used in *On Their Own* per pair

Small cups, 1 per pair

Big cups, or bottom halves of milk cartons, labeled with a number corresponding to the number of red blocks that would fill the cup to the top,
1 per pair

Overview

Children use strategies to predict which of three kinds of Pattern Blocks can be used to fill a cup with a specified number of blocks. In this activity, children have the opportunity to:

- ◆ make and revise estimates
- ◆ count and compare amounts
- ◆ measure volume

The Activity

Introducing

- ◆ Before children come together, determine how many red trapezoids will fill the small cup. Keep that number to yourself.
- ◆ Distribute a small cup, two triangles, two trapezoids, and two hexagons to each pair of children.
- ◆ Tell children that it is possible to fill the cup in front of them with approximately ——— of one of these three kinds of blocks (give whatever number you determined for the trapezoids.) Ask pairs to use the blocks you gave them to help try to decide which kind would fill the cup with that number of blocks.
- ◆ Call on volunteers to give their predictions, and to explain how they made them.
- ◆ Distribute more triangles, trapezoids, and hexagons, and suggest that children now check their predictions by filling the cup with blocks. Have children compare their predictions to their findings.
- ◆ Confirm that the cup holds about ——— (give the number counted) red trapezoids.

©ETA/Cuisenaire®

On Their Own

> **Which kind of block will fill the big cup to the top—red, green or yellow?**
>
> - Work with a partner.
>
> - The number on the big cup tells how many Pattern Blocks of one kind would fill the big cup. Predict whether that number of red, green, or yellow Pattern Blocks would fill the big cup.
>
> - Use blocks to find the answer. You won't have enough to actually fill the cup, so you and your partner will have to find another way to figure out the answer.
>
> - Be ready to explain how you decided on your answer.

The Bigger Picture

Thinking and Sharing

Invite children to share their answers and describe their strategies. You may wish to record children's predictions on the chalkboard. Then distribute enough Pattern Blocks so several pairs of children can fill their cups completely with red, green, or yellow blocks, and then count to find out what kind of block corresponds with the number on the cup.

Use prompts like these to promote class discussion:

- How did you decide which color block fills the cup?

- Are there any other methods you can think of for finding an answer when you don't have enough blocks to fill the big cup?

- When the big cups were filled with blocks, did the number of blocks exactly match the number on the cup? Why might they be different?

- If you were asked to guess the number of tan blocks that would fill the cup, do you think it would be greater than or less than the number of red blocks? Why?

Extending the Activity

Have children use the results of the activity to estimate the number of blue blocks that the cup would hold. Then have them use blue blocks to check their estimates.

Where's the Mathematics?

This activity helps children to develop number sense based on proportional reasoning. Because they are not at first given enough Pattern Blocks to fill their cup, children have an opportunity to think logically on the basis of partial data. For example, a child might reason, "Ten red blocks filled half the cup. So I'll need 10 more blocks to fill the cup. That means it will take 20 red blocks to fill the cup. Twenty is pretty close to the 18 written on the cup, so I think red blocks is the answer." Another child might figure, "Fifteen triangles didn't fill even half the cup. It says 18 blocks filled the cup, so it couldn't be triangles."

Children may ask whether they should pack the Pattern Blocks as neatly and closely as possible or whether they should just drop a handful of Pattern Blocks into the cup. If they pack the blocks compactly, children will find that they are able to put in the most blocks, whereas simply dropping in a handful allows more empty space to occupy the cup. Regardless of how they pack the blocks, children come to an intuitive understanding of volume as a quantitative measure of space. They are sure to find that the smallest shape—the triangle—can be packed with the least amount of empty space around it, whereas the largest shape—the hexagon—is likely to have the most space around it.

This activity also gives children an opportunity to develop an understanding of the blocks' relative sizes. Children can discover that the number of red blocks needed to fill the cup is less than the number of green blocks but greater than the number of yellow blocks needed. This realization may lead some children to generalize that the smaller the block, the greater the number of blocks needed to fill the cup. Some may be able to associate specific numbers with this concept: For example, it takes two red trapezoids to cover the yellow hexagon; therefore, one should be able to fit about twice as many trapezoids as hexagons into the cup. Likewise, it takes six triangles to cover the yellow hexagon, so one should be able to fit six times as many triangles as hexagons into the cup. Using this logic, children may reason that if the cup holds 10 hexagons, it should hold 10 + 10, or 20, trapezoids, and 10 + 10 + 10 + 10 + 10 + 10, or 60, triangles. Using this idea of relative size can help children to conclude that more tan blocks than red blocks can fill the cup. However, many young children may not be ready to do this kind of reasoning without first filling the cup with the different blocks, counting the different amounts, and looking at the results.

During the class discussion, children may find that the number of blocks that they are able to fit in the cup may be slightly different from the one you wrote on the label of the cup. There is also likely to be a range of numbers when you poll the class about their results. The fact that the results vary can be used to help children appreciate the inexact nature of some measuring techniques.

SCOOP AND SORT

• Counting
• Comparing
• Graphing

Getting Ready

What You'll Need

Pattern Blocks, 8 of each shape per group

Buckets or large baggies for Pattern Blocks, 1 per group

Newsprint (12" x 18" pieces) folded into 6 columns and 9 rows, with a Pattern Block shape outline at the top of each column, 2 sheets per pair

Overview

Children take random samples of Pattern Blocks, sort them, and record their results. In this activity, children have the opportunity to:

◆ sort and classify shapes

◆ organize information in a graph

◆ compare numbers

◆ make generalizations

The Activity

Children are likely to suggest sorting blocks according to color. However, they may suggest other methods such as sorting by number of corners (vertices) or number of sides.

Introducing

◆ Put a bucket of Pattern Blocks in a central location.

◆ Invite a few volunteers, one at a time, to scoop up a handful of blocks and count them. Point out that the number of blocks differ, and invite children to speculate about why.

◆ Ask children how the blocks in any handful might be sorted. Establish that one way would be to put all the blocks with the same shape together.

On Their Own

What can you discover about a handful of Pattern Blocks?

- Work with a partner. One of you scoop up some Pattern Blocks.

- Sort the blocks so the same shapes are together.

- Arrange the blocks on one of the large sheets of newsprint. Put all the same kind of block in the same column, 1 in a box.

- Record your results on another large sheet of newsprint.

- What information does your picture give? Think about ways you can compare the numbers of blocks in each column.

The Bigger Picture

Thinking and Sharing

Post a volunteer's graph on the chalkboard and ask the class to make statements about the results.

Use prompts such as these to promote class discussion:

- How many blocks did you scoop up?

- What did you notice when you looked at your graph?

- On the graph that is posted, are there more blue blocks or red blocks? How do you know?

- Does that graph show fewer green blocks or tan blocks? How many fewer? How do you know?

- Which column has three (four, five) more blocks than another column?

- Compare the column of orange blocks with the column of green blocks. Can you think of two different ways to give your answer?

- Which column has the most blocks? the fewest blocks?

Writing

Have partners write as many statements as they can about the data shown on their Pattern Block graph.

Extending the Activity

1. Post three graphs for which children wrote statements. Read the statements written about one of the graphs, and have the class decide to which graph the statements refer.

2. Create a list of statements about a Pattern Block graph. Then have the class work together to create a graph that matches the statements.

Where's the Mathematics?

Using a graph as a visual way of organizing and presenting data is an important mathematical concept, and using and interpreting data from a situation that children have created themselves is meaningful and motivational. Children can see that their graph helps them to answer questions such as "Do you have more blue or more green shapes?" or "Which child had the most red trapezoids?" more efficiently than by looking at Pattern Blocks piled in a heap on their desks.

As children sort their scoops of Pattern Blocks, you may overhear comments such as, "Oooh, look at all the blue I got," or "I've got more reds than you do," or "All the green ones are triangles." Seeing these observations translated into symbols and organized into a graph helps children understand the power of mathematics as a tool of organization.

When children compare columns on the graph, they are gaining experience using phrases such as "more than," "less than," and "is the same as" to express comparisons. For example, in describing the graph below, children may say that "the number of tan shapes is the same as the number of yellow shapes," or that "the number of triangles is less than the number of squares."

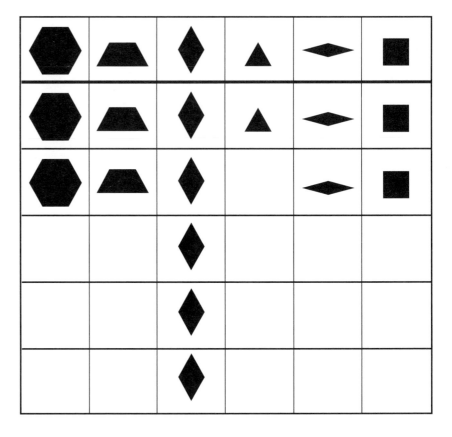

In addition, some children may grasp the concept that a comparison of two numbers can be made in more than one way. For example, stating that "the number of tan shapes is greater than the number of green shapes" or "the number of green shapes is less than the number of tan shapes" is saying virtually the same thing.

Children use various methods to compare the quantities shown in the graph. When asked to tell which column has a greater number of blocks, some children count and compare the number of shapes in each column, while others make the comparison visually, checking to see which column is longer. Similarly, when asked to find out how many more blues than reds there are, children use different strategies. Some count each column and then subtract two from five, whereas others use the method of "counting on," matching up the two columns and counting "1, 2, 3" to find out the number of extra pieces in the blue column.

Asking questions such as "How many more blue blocks were scooped than red blocks?" or "How many blocks did (child's name) pick up in his/her scoop?" requires children to do additional subtraction and addition computation. This enables children to learn that graphs often include embedded information requiring more analysis than the casual visual inspection needed to answer the question "Does the graph show fewer green blocks or tan blocks?"

Some children may use the geometric names of the blocks, rather than colors, to describe their graphs. Many children are familiar with the terms *triangle* and *square*, but not with the terms *parallelogram, rhombus, trapezoid,* or *hexagon,* so you are apt to hear "There are more yellow shapes than triangles." Children may use this opportunity to ask about the names of the shapes with which they are not familiar.

This activity may also reinforce children's understanding of the concept of zero. If a child fails to scoop any blocks of a given kind, he or she has a column that is a graphic representation of zero. The child may then be able to make generalizations about, and comparisons involving, a set that consists of zero objects.

Grappling with the answers to the questions "Did everyone pick up the same number of blocks? Why or why not?" touches on the concept of sampling variability, which figures prominently in the area of statistics. Children may also note that tan rhombuses take up less room; therefore, if a child scooped up a lot of tan shapes, he or she probably had a larger number of blocks than the child who scooped up more yellow hexagons.

SPIN AND GRAPH

- Counting
- Sorting
- Graphing
- Chance

Getting Ready

What You'll Need

Pattern Blocks, 10 each of green, red, and orange per pair

Spin and Graph spinner, page 95

Long sheets of paper

Overhead Pattern Blocks (optional)

Overview

Children use a spinner with different sectors allocated to three different Pattern Blocks and keep track of how many times each shape comes up within a specific number of spins. In this activity, children have the opportunity to:

◆ organize and graph data

◆ associate the size of a sector on a spinner with the likelihood of its coming up

The Activity

You may wish to display the graph recording sheet as an overhead transparency or you may want to display a large floor model of it.

Introducing

◆ Display the *Spin and Graph* spinner. Invite children to describe what they see and how they might use the spinner.

◆ Explain to children that they are going to use the spinner to get information to record on a graph.

◆ Show children a graph recording sheet with these headings:

◆ Call on a volunteer to spin the spinner. Call on another volunteer to place a Pattern Block in the column that corresponds to the shape that comes up on the spinner.

◆ Call on some more volunteers to spin the spinner and place Pattern Blocks on the graph.

©ETA/Cuisenaire®

On Their Own

Can you predict which Pattern Block shape will come up most often on a spinner?

- Work with a partner. Share a spinner and a graph sheet like these.

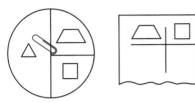

- Decide which shape on the spinner will be the first to come up 10 times. Write down your guess.

- Then take turns spinning the spinner. For each spin, place a block on the graph sheet.

- Keep taking turns until there are 10 blocks in 1 column on the graph sheet.

- Compare your guess with what happened. Be ready to talk about what you see.

The Bigger Picture

Thinking and Sharing

Ask for volunteers to bring up their graphs and report their results. Display each graph for all to see. Then transfer each pair's findings to a larger graph.

Use prompts like these to promote class discussion:

- What did you notice about your results?

- Whose spins turned out the way they thought they would? Why do you think that was?

- What does the class graph show about the shape with the most spins?

- How does the class graph compare to your own?

- Would you call the spinner a "fair" spinner? Explain.

Extending the Activity

Have children repeat the activity after creating a new face for their spinner using any three kinds of Pattern Blocks and any allotment of space they like.

Where's the Mathematics?

This activity introduces children to topics in probability. It also provides children with an opportunity to make connections among various areas of mathematics in that it has them use some geometric vocabulary, make a graph that involves counting and comparing skills, and do intuitive work with fractions.

Many children are familiar with using spinners from board games that they have played at home. Typically, those spinners are divided into equal sectors and offer a "fair chance" of stopping on any given sector. Having a "fair chance" is what makes the game fun to play.

The spinner used in this activity is not fair. The chances of the spinner stopping on the green triangle are twice as great as stopping on the orange square or red trapezoid. Many children will not recognize this fact just by looking at the spinner. They will have to work through this activity and then during the class discussion reflect on why so many of their classmates' graphs had more green triangles than trapezoids or squares.

When children are initially asked to predict which column they think will fill first, many will pick their favorite shape or favorite color without observing the effect that the relative sizes of the sectors might have on the outcome. In fact, if you were to repeat this activity several days or weeks later, some children would still predict their favorite shape or color as the column to fill first. Only frequent experience with chance events over time can help them solidify their grasp of probability.

Although the unfair spinner makes the lesson focus on chance events, children get needed practice in collecting, organizing, and analyzing data. Young children gain experience with concrete graphs as they touch and manipulate actual objects to create their graphs. Watching how the pooling of information creates one large class graph that mimics the shape of many of the individual graphs can be an interesting revelation to these children.

Later, as they become more sophisticated, children can move to more representational or abstract graphing.

There are two types of probability that are touched on in the activity: experimental and theoretical. Experimental probability is what actually happens. Children engage in experimental probability as they use the spinners, collect their data, and make their graphs. During the first four spins, children might spin trapezoid, square, triangle, and trapezoid in which case the experimental probability of spinning a triangle is 1 out of 4 or ¼. Theoretical probability is what is likely to happen based on a great deal of data. When the children pool their collective data and make one large classroom graph and analyze it, they will be moving toward theoretical probability. For the spinner used in this activity, the theoretical probability of it landing on a green triangle is 1 out of 2 or ½ because the green triangle sector is ½ of the entire area of the spinner; so theoretically, one would expect the spinner to land on the green triangle twice if the spinner were spun four times. Frequently, the experimental probability of just a few spins does not exactly match the theoretical probability one would predict as the outcome. In later grades, children will learn that theoretical probability assumes that the spinner has been spun hundreds, or even thousands, of times.

Theoretically, them, half the spin will be green triangles. But the question is not "Which block will be spun the most?" but "Which block will be the first to be spun 10 times?" As it happens, the theoretical probability that the first block to reach 10 spins is much more than half; in theory, the triangle will win about 88% of the time. Children's responses may not reflect this figure, though, because 12 experiments is till a small sample space. Repeating the activity another time or two and continuing to add the results on the the original class graph will give results that will more closely align with what is theoretically supposed to happen.

SPIN TO WIN

- Spatial visualization
- Properties of geometric shapes
- Game strategies
- Equivalence

Getting Ready

What You'll Need

Pattern blocks, about 30 per team

Spin to Win game board, page 96

Spin To Win spinner, page 97

Overhead Pattern Blocks (optional)

Overview

Children play a game in which they spin for Pattern Blocks, and use the indicated Pattern Blocks or an equivalent combination of blocks to cover a game board. In this activity, children have the opportunity to:

- ◆ develop spatial reasoning
- ◆ find combinations of shapes that will cover a region
- ◆ develop strategic thinking skills

The Activity

Introducing

- ◆ Display a red trapezoid. Ask volunteers to show how smaller shapes could be put together to cover the shape.

- ◆ Show children the spinner. Have volunteers spin the spinner to get shapes that would cover the red trapezoid.

     ©ETA/Cuisenaire®

On Their Own

Play *Spin to Win!*

Here are the rules.

1. This is a game for 2 teams of 2 players each. The object is to cover a game board with Pattern Blocks. Each team gets a game board that looks like this:

2. Teams take turns spinning the spinner.

3. When a team takes its turn, it has two choices:
   - The team may take the block that comes up on the spinner and place it on the game board.
   - The team may take smaller blocks that can be put together to make the block that comes up and then place those smaller blocks on the game board.

4. Once a team has placed blocks on the game board, they cannot be moved.

5. If a team cannot fit a block it spins on the game board, that team loses its turn.

6. The team that covers its game board first is the winner.

- Play several games of *Spin to Win*.
- Be ready to talk about good moves and bad moves.

The Bigger Picture

Thinking and Sharing

Invite children to talk about their games and describe some of the thinking they did.

Use prompts such as these to promote class discussion.

- How did you decide where to put your blocks?
- Did your strategy change as the board became closer to being full? If so, how?
- Did you ever choose smaller blocks when you spun larger ones? Why or why not?
- Did you make any moves that you wanted to take back? Explain.
- What are some blocks that you used instead of the yellow hexagon? instead of the red trapezoid?
- Which blocks did you find most difficult to use? Why? What strategies did you use to help you place these blocks?
- What strategies did you use to help you win?

Drawing

Have children choose a favorite winning board, trace the pieces, and color them.

Extending the Activity

1. Have children play a variation of the game in which they are not allowed to trade larger blocks for smaller ones. Ask children if they think this version of game is easier or more difficult than the original game. Then have them tell you which version they prefer, and why.

Teacher Talk

Where's the Mathematics?

In the course of playing this game, children will be recognizing how shapes can be rotated or flipped to fit into specific spots, developing logical thinking skills, and learning to visualize and think ahead in anticipation of what might happen next.

During the early part of the game, children are likely to take the exact piece shown on the spinner. Toward the end of the game, as the board fills up and smaller empty spaces are left, they will be forced to think about trading. For example, if the game board looks like this and children spin a trapezoid, their initial reaction might be that the turn has been lost because the trapezoid cannot be played.

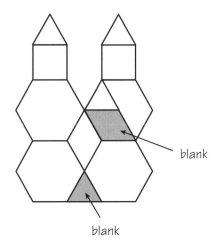

blank

blank

You may have to step in and remind the children that they can trade in the trapezoid for smaller pieces and encourage them to see that three green triangles or a green triangle and a blue parallelogram can be used to form the trapezoid. They do not have to place the triangle and parallelogram on the game board as a trapezoid; they may place the two pieces in separate spots on the game board. They must, however, use both pieces on their turn so that they have placed the equivalent of the trapezoid that they spun. As children play the game, they discover that many different combinations of shapes can be used to cover a region. They also recognize that shapes can be rotated or flipped to fit into specific spots. For example, the blank region on the game board on the following page can be covered by a variety of arrangements, some of which are shown to the right of the board.

©ETA/Cuisenaire®

2. Have children play a variation of the game in which in place of a turn, they may trade a larger block that is already on the game board for smaller blocks. Ask children if they think this version of game is easier or more difficult than the original game. Then have them tell you which version they prefer, and why.

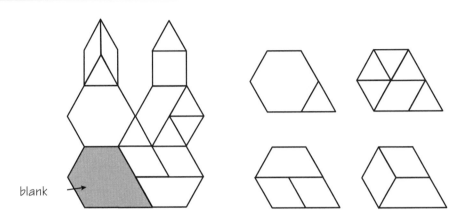

blank

When discussing the strategies they developed, children are apt to note that the yellow hexagon, green triangle, red trapezoid, and blue parallelogram are easier to play than the orange square and tan rhombus because the first four pieces form quite a few interchangeable combinations while the square and tan rhombus do not fit completely on top of any of the other Pattern Blocks. The square and tan rhombus can only be used on the "towers" of the game board. Using them anywhere else will lead to odd spaces that cannot be filled at the end of the game.

Children may also tell you they like to spin the larger shapes—hexagon and trapezoid—at the beginning of the game when lots of area needs to be covered and then spin the smaller shapes—blue parallelogram and triangle— towards the end of the game when smaller amounts of area need to be covered. Even though the hexagon and trapezoid may be traded in for the smaller pieces, spinning one of these shapes at the end of the game may still leave them with too many small pieces and result in a lost turn.

This game develops children's ability to visualize how larger shapes may be broken down into smaller shapes. This skill will help them later when they discuss fractions and learn to recognize situations in which one piece represents a fractional part of another; for example, the blue parallelogram is 2/3 of a red trapezoid. Children will also use this skill when they are confronted with finding the area of a complex shape and need to break the shape down into smaller areas that they may work with more easily. Although children will not encounter such applications for many years, providing the hands-on experiences in the primary grades establishes a firm foundation for later teachers to build on.

THINGS WITH LEGS

Getting Ready

What You'll Need

Pattern Blocks, about 20 per child
drawing paper
Pattern Block stickers (optional)
Pattern Blocks shapes, page 98
Overhead Pattern Blocks (optional)
Glue (optional)
Clothespins (optional)
Rope or string (optional)

Overview

Children give their imaginative talents free rein as they use Pattern Blocks to create pictures of anything that has legs. Then they sort their pictures and post them as a graph. In this activity, children have the opportunity to:

- ◆ make a paper-and pencil representation of Pattern Block shapes

- ◆ sort and classify shapes

- ◆ organize and analyze information on a graph

The Activity

There are several ways children can transfer their Pattern Block designs to paper. You may wish to have them use Pattern Block stickers, glue Pattern Blocks shapes made from colored construction paper, or trace the blocks and color in the design.

Introducing

- • Explain to children that today the Pattern Blocks will become their tools for creating a design.

- • Call on a volunteer to use two or more Pattern Blocks to create a design.

- • Show children how to transfer the design to paper.

©ETA/Cuisenaire®

On Their Own

Use as many Pattern Blocks as you like to make a picture of something that has legs.

- *Try making different pictures of things with legs until you find something that you really like.*

- *Then transfer your Pattern Block picture to paper.*

- *Share your pictures with each other.*

The Bigger Picture

Thinking and Sharing

Ask two children to show their pictures and to tell how they are alike and different. Then have another child share his or her design and compare it to the other two pictures. After all of the art has been displayed, ask the class for ideas on how to sort the pictures into groups in order to create a graph. For example, the pictures might be sorted by the number or kind of Pattern Blocks used or by descriptive words—for example, *People, Animals, Furniture*. Make labels based on the categories suggested by the class. Post each label at the left side of a row. Then invite children to place their pictures in the appropriate rows. Add categories if necessary. Continue the process until all of the pictures are posted.

One way to display the graph is to put up horizontal, parallel lengths of rope or string and use clothespins to attach the pictures to the ropes. This creates a graph that can be easily moved around and changed.

Use prompts like these to promote class discussion.

- What do you notice as you look at the graph?

- How many rows are on the graph?

- Which row has the most pictures? fewest pictures?

- How many more _____ are there than _____ ? How do you know this?

- Are there more pictures of living things or things made by people? How many more? How do you know this?

- Do any of the pictures have symmetry in them? Which ones?

Drawing and Writing

Ask children to make a list of other categories they could have used to sort these pictures.

Extending the Activity

1. Have children choose different categories and resort the pictures.

Where's the Mathematics?

In this activity children are encouraged to be imaginative both in the designs they create and in the categories they suggest for the sorting part of the activity. Since the topic "Things with Legs" suggests many things that the children see everyday in the world around them, they should have a wealth of ideas to translate into Pattern Block art.

As children transfer their designs to paper, they practice using 2-dimensional shapes to represent 3-dimensional figures, and gain experience in establishing a 1:1 correspondence between the block designs and the representations of those designs on paper. Finer motor control is required when using the stickers, cutouts, or tracing than when using the blocks.

As children suggest and use rules for sorting their designs, they identify attributes and use these attributes to create a graph. After all the sorting rules have been offered, the discussion that leads to selection of one of the rules for the class to use for their graph will involve additional value judgments as children offer reasons, such as, "Using the number of legs is an easy rule because you only have to count, but the rule about whether the design could be made only of trapezoids is too hard."

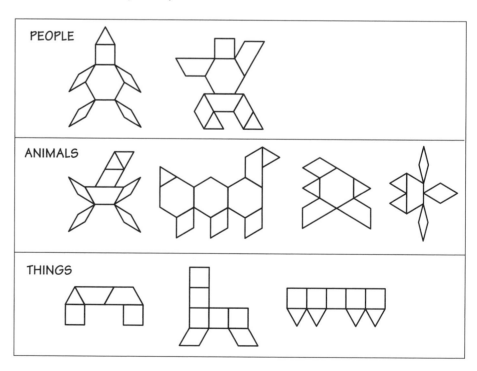

2. Collect children's topic suggestions and use some or all of these to repeat the activity.

In the process of talking about the data they have posted, children count, combine, and compare numerical data and thereby deepen their number sense. Questions such as "Are there more pictures of living things or things made by people?" require children to use higher order thinking skills as they sort each category into "living things" and "non-living things," and then have to find each total and compare those two totals before they reach a final answer. When children notice that people (as one example) don't all look alike, yet are all grouped together on the graph, children learn more about making generalizations.

Answering the question "Do any of the pictures have symmetry in them?" gives children the opportunity to focus on one of the properties of geometric figures. They may enjoy using a ruler to indicate where the lines of symmetry may be found.

THREE IN A ROW

• **Properties of geometric shapes**
• **Spatial reasoning**

Getting Ready

What You'll Need

Pattern Blocks

Books, boxes, or other barriers

Overhead Pattern Blocks (optional)

Overview

Children take turns making secret designs with three Pattern Blocks and describing them to their partners, who try to make the designs from the clues they are given. In this activity, children have the opportunity to:

◆ communicate about geometric designs

◆ think about how to improve their verbal descriptions

◆ use directional words in context

◆ follow a set of directions

The Activity

You might want to put the pieces on the overhead projector but not turn the projector on.

Introducing

◆ Prepare a design like the one shown, and keep it hidden. Tell children you want them to listen to clues about the design you have made with your Pattern Blocks.

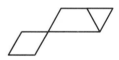

◆ Give one descriptive clue about your design, for example, "My design has one triangle, one red, and one blue shape." Then ask children to try to make your design with their Pattern Blocks.

◆ Observe children's designs. Point out that you see many designs that follow your first clue, but that not all of them look like *your* design.

◆ Give another clue, for example, "One side of my triangle lines up exactly with a short side on the red shape." Allow time for the children to rearrange their Pattern Blocks, if necessary, to fit this clue.

◆ Repeat this process, giving additional clues, such as, "My triangle is on the far right of my design," "The red shape is in the middle and the longest side of the red shape is on the bottom," and "Just the corner of the blue shape touches the lower lefthand corner of the red shape."

◆ Continue giving clues and allowing children to change their designs until their designs match yours, and are in the same orientation as yours. Then, display your design.

©ETA/Cuisenaire®

On Their Own

Can you describe your Pattern Block design so your partner can make it, too?

- Work with a partner. One of you make a secret design using 3 Pattern Blocks. The blocks must touch.

- The partner who makes the secret design gives the other partner a clue about the design so that he or she can try to make the same design with Pattern Blocks.

- One clue will not be enough. So the partner who made the design must give more clues, 1 at a time.

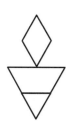

- Here's an example of clues for this design.

  Clue 1: It has 1 blue shape, 1 red shape, and 1 green shape.

  Clue 2: The red shape is in the middle, with the longest side on top.

  Clue 3: One of the sharp points of the blue shape stands on top of the red shape.

  Clue 4: The green shape is under the red shape, and together the two shapes form a triangle.

- When the partner thinks he or she has enough clues and hs made the design, check to see if your designs match!

- Take turns making shapes and following clues.

The Bigger Picture

Thinking and Sharing

Invite pairs to discuss their experiences both describing designs and following directions. Have some pairs draw their last design on the chalkboard.

Use prompts like these to promote class discussion:

- What was difficult about this activity? What was easy?

- What are some of the directions you used to describe the way the blocks in your design were placed?

- How could you describe how the blocks in the posted design are arranged?

- Is there another way to describe how the blocks are arranged?

Writing

Have the class generate a list of useful phrases that could be used when giving clues. For example, they might include above, to the left, the corners just touch, and so forth.

Where's the Mathematics?

This activity dramatizes for children the need for precise communication about geometric shapes. When children give clues to their partners, they receive immediate feedback on whether a clue is helpful or not. If the partner hearing a clue interprets it with his or her Pattern Blocks as intended, it can be considered to be a good clue. If not, the child giving the clue needs to figure out what additional information is needed to clarify the situation.

When children begin this activity, they are apt to use simple directions. For example, a child may say, "I put the blue block above the red block." They soon learn that their partners may interpret this direction in many different ways. Here are just a few examples of how this direction could be interpreted:

The child giving the directions quickly learns from his or her partner that more detail is necessary. For example, in order to help his or her partner to produce the first design shown, the child may revise the directions: "Put the blue block next to the top of red block so that the two sides line up exactly. Oh, and make sure the top of the blue block points to the right."

Extending the Activity

Have children use three to five blocks to make a secret design. Children should then trace around the design, and color in each block. When they are finished, children provide partners with written or oral directions on how to produce the design. The partners follow the directions and compare their designs to the originals.

Key phrases, such as *left side, top right hand corner, bottom side, above,* and *below* all are likely to be used by children. Some children in the primary grades still have difficulty with the meanings of these directional words. As children work together, they practice using such words, and soon know whether they were used and interpreted correctly.

Children are apt to be surprised by how many clues they have to give. It takes a lot of words to describe one simple design accurately. Children may also find that clues they gave earlier are ignored or forgotten as their partners try to deal with the information they receive in later clues.

You may be amused to hear some creative descriptions thrown in among more precise language clues. For example, one child described the following design as a "chicken with a baseball cap on."

Children often report that the more they did this activity, the easier it became. Partners develop a repertoire of clues that they both understand and thus spend less time clarifying each step of the description.

WHO AM I?

- **Properties of geometric shapes**
- **Spatial reasoning**
- **Following directions**

Getting Ready

What You'll Need

Pattern Blocks, 1 set of 6 per pair
Overhead Pattern Blocks (optional)

Overview

Children create a Pattern Block design, then find a way to describe one block in their design in such a way that other children can use the description to identify that block. In this activity, children have the opportunity to:

- ◆ use attributes other than color to identify shapes
- ◆ determine relevant information
- ◆ use deductive reasoning

The Activity

Introducing

- ◆ Show children this Pattern Block design.
- ◆ Explain that you are going to pretend to be one of the three blocks in this design. Tell children that you will describe yourself, and would like children to pick out the block that you are pretending to be.
- ◆ Give the following clues, pausing after each to give children a moment to work with the clue: "I have four sides. I am not the biggest block. I am at the top of the design. Who am I?"
- ◆ After children have identified the blue block, point out that you did not use color in your description because it would have given away the answer too soon. Then call on a few volunteers to pretend to be one of the blocks and to give clues to his or her identity. Help children to model their descriptions after yours giving a few clues and then asking, "Who am I?"

On Their Own

Can you describe 1 block in your Pattern Block design so other children can figure out which block you are describing?

- Work with a partner. Choose 4 or 5 Pattern Blocks and use them to make a design on a piece of paper.

- Trace around the blocks in your design.

- Together, choose 1 of the blocks in your design. Pretend you are that block. Write a description of yourself so that other children looking at your design will be able to figure out who you are. Do not include your color in your description!

- When everyone is ready, exchange designs and descriptions with another pair of children. Try to figure out which block each pair has described.

The Bigger Picture

Thinking and Sharing

Invite pairs of children to post their designs and present their clues for the class to solve.

Use prompts like these to promote class discussion:

- Which did you like more, writing clues or solving puzzles? Why?
- When you were trying to identify another pair's block, were all the clues helpful? Why or why not?
- Did you need all of the clues? Could you have used more clues? Explain.
- Do you have enough information to solve this posted design? If not, what clue could you add?

Extending the Activity

Have children use three or four Pattern Block shapes to make a design. Children can then make up a riddle in which the clues tell how many blocks are in the design, and how many green blocks it takes to cover the design. From these clues, other children can try to guess which shapes are in the design.

Where's the Mathematics?

This activity helps children focus on the attributes of the Pattern Blocks. As they write their description of the block they have chosen, children need to look closely at their design to determine whether they have included enough discriminating information. For example, the clue that "a block has four sides" correctly describes the red trapezoid, blue parallelogram, tan rhombus, and the orange square. Even a more refined clue that "all four sides are the same length" still includes the parallelogram, the rhombus, and the square. In order to allow other children to correctly identify a shape, a clue must offer additional information about the angles or the position of the block in the design.

Some children may have particular difficulty writing complete descriptions. One child, for example, might write:

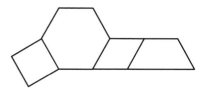

I have 4 sides.
I come after the hexagon.
Who am I?

These clues eliminate the square, but still leave it unclear whether the solution is the parallelogram or the trapezoid. Children may need to read each clue and test whether different blocks fit the clue in order to see that they have not given enough information for the other children to identify the intended block. Or the clue giver may need to clarify some of the terms: For example, "after" might need to become "immediately after."

Some children may write clues that include redundant information:

I have 6 sides.
I am the largest shape in the design.
I touch all of the other shapes in the design.
Who am I?

Since the directions to this activity did not rule out redundancy, this child is to be commended for his or her eye to detail!

I come after the second shape.
I have 3 sides.
Who am I?

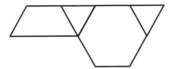

The next set of clues contains the positional word "after" and the ordinal "second." These both are key ideas for young children.

By calling children's attention to how language such as "above," "below," "to the right," and "on the left" help them to write meaningful clues, you are providing an important lesson in communication. As children share their clues and identify each other's secret block, they are reinforcing the correct use of such terms. (If children say "right" when they mean "left," the chances are that their peers will correct them.)

Some children may write relatively sophisticated clues, embedding in them such critical geometric concepts as *comparison* or *area*. Children may also use negative statements, specifying what the shape is not. For example:

It takes fewer than 3 triangles to cover me.
I am not a square.
Who am I?

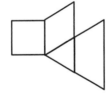

Certain children may have difficulty with clues written in the negative form, such as "I am not a square." These children may find it helpful to cover up the square with their hand as a way of eliminating it from the field of possible solutions.

As you discuss the clues with the class and have children answer the questions "Which shapes did this clue help you rule out? Why?" and "Do we have enough information to solve this puzzle? If not, what clue could we add?", you will be strengthening children's deductive reasoning skills. You will also be encouraging children to read carefully and to think things through.

WHO CAUGHT THE BIGGER FISH?

- Area
- Comparing
- Counting
- Equivalence

Getting Ready

What You'll Need

Pattern Blocks, a set of at least 8 hexagons, 16 trapezoids, 23 blue parallelograms, and 50 green triangles per pair

Fish outlines, pages 99 and 100, 1 each per pair

Overhead Pattern Blocks (optional)

Overview

Children use Pattern Blocks to compare the areas of two fish shapes and decide which is bigger. In this activity, children have the opportunity to:

- ◆ measure area in non-standard units
- ◆ discover methods for comparing area
- ◆ discover that when the unit of measurement is the same, comparisons are more easily made

The Activity

As children explain which shape they think is bigger, make a list on the board of some of the words they use such as long, short, tall, big, small, wide.

Introducing

- ◆ Show children the outlines of two shapes made from Pattern Blocks.
- ◆ Ask them which shape they think is bigger and why.
- ◆ Explain that one way to figure out which shape is bigger is to find out how much space each covers. Then cover the first shape with blue parallelograms.
- ◆ Ask a volunteer to cover the second shape with blue parallelograms. Ask the class to tell which shape is bigger and why.

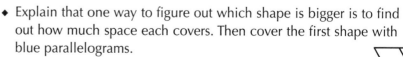

©ETA/Cuisenaire®

On Their Own

Who caught the bigger fish, John or Carol?

- Work with your partner. Use an outline of John's Fish and an outline of Carol's fish. Here are pictures of the outlines.

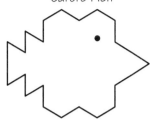
Carol's Fish

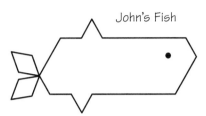
John's Fish

- Use Pattern Blocks to cover each fish to help find its size.

- Keep track of the type and number of Pattern Blocks that you used.

- Figure out which fish is bigger. Be ready to explain your answer.

- Think of ways to describe how much bigger the bigger fish is.

The Bigger Picture

Thinking and Sharing

Invite children to discuss how they found the sizes of the fish. As children discuss results, record the numbers of blocks that children used on the board.

Use prompts like these to promote class discussion.

- What method did you use for comparing the two fish?

- Which fish is bigger? How do you know?

- Did anyone have a different answer? What is it?

- Here is one set of blocks for how big John's (Carol's) fish is, and here is a different set of blocks for how big John's (Carol's) fish is. Does this mean the same fish has different sizes? Explain.

- How much bigger is the bigger fish? How do you know?

Extending the Activity

Have pairs of children create two new fish using Pattern Blocks. Then have them trace around the two outlines. Ask them to guess which fish is larger. Then have them check their guesses by using Pattern Blocks to measure and compare the fish.

Where's the Mathematics?

This activity helps children develop an informal understanding of the concept of area. In the problem, Carol's fish is slightly larger in area than John's. Her fish measures 48 triangular units, while John's fish can be covered with 46 triangles. Children may have used Pattern Blocks other than the triangle to make their area measurements, but they should arrive at the same conclusion that Carol's fish is slightly larger.

Although this problem has only one correct answer, it is open-ended in the sense that children may use a variety of methods for measuring and comparing the two fish. Some children may fill in the first outline with a combination of Pattern Blocks, then try to use the same blocks to cover the second outline. These children will express their measurements as a combination of blocks.

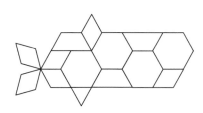

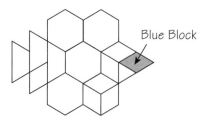

Blue Block

I used these blocks to fill John's fish.

    4 yellow blocks

    3 red blocks

    6 blue blocks

    1 green block

I put the same blocks in Carol's fish.

Carol's fish still had room for 1 blue block or 2 green blocks.

Carol's fish is 1 blue block bigger than John's fish.

Carol's fish is 2 green blocks bigger than John's fish.

As they experiment, some children may decide that using only one type of Pattern Block is easier. These children will find that while John's fish can be covered completely by either triangles or blue parallelograms, Carol's fish can be completely covered by triangles or trapezoids.

Asking children to decide whether two seemingly different measurements given by class members are really the same or not is apt to lead to a discussion of converting everything to one type of Pattern Block so that comparisons may be more easily made. Some children who began by using many different types of blocks and then decided to express their answers using only triangles may be able to use equivalencies among the blocks to figure out the number of triangles needed without actually covering the fish with triangles. For example, if they used 4 hexagons and recognize that 6 triangles cover a hexagon, they can use addition to find that the area covered by 4 hexagons is equivalent to 6 + 6 + 6 + 6, or 24, triangles. They could make similar conversions using 1 trapezoid = 3 triangles or 1 parallelogram = 2 triangles.

This idea of equivalency is a key one in mathematics. You can help make connections for children by pointing out that this is the same idea we use when we convert 2 feet to 24 inches, substitute 5 nickels for l quarter, or trade in ten units for one rod when using place value manipulatives. Children will use equivalency later when they study fractions and learn that 1 = 3/3 or 1 = 2/2. They are seeing this same idea when they work with the idea that one trapezoid = 3 triangles and one parallelogram = 2 triangles.

Children in later grades often respond to the question, "What is area?" with the answer that area is length times width. This dependency on an algorithm may indicate that they do not really understand that area implies the amount of surface covered by a shape. Giving children opportunities to find the area of irregular shapes by covering them up with Pattern Blocks will help to deepen their understanding of the concept of area. Finally, listening to each other explain their strategies in approaching this problem will give them an appreciation for the fact that one may arrive at an answer through many different ways.

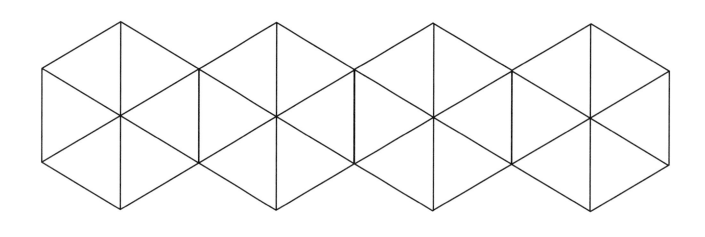

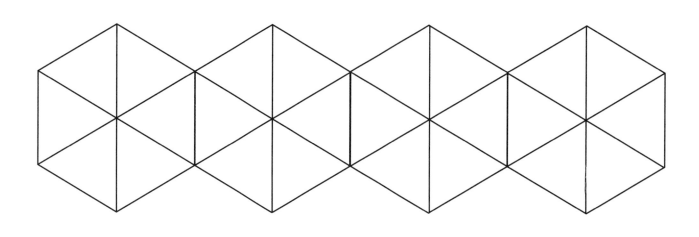

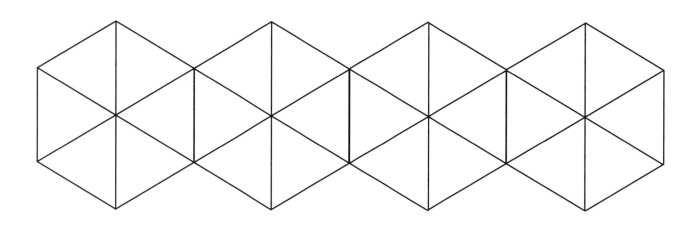

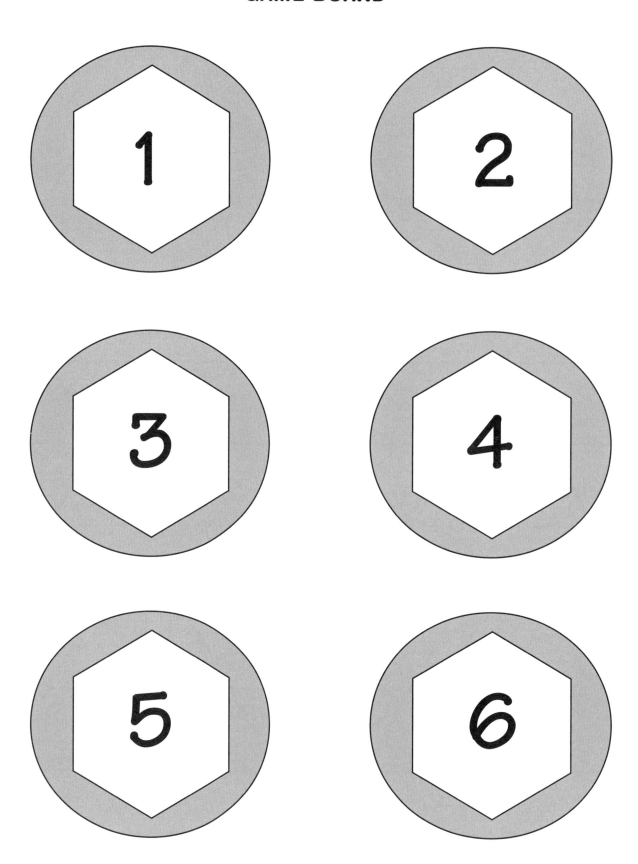

PATTERN BLOCK PIZZA
TOPPING SPINNER

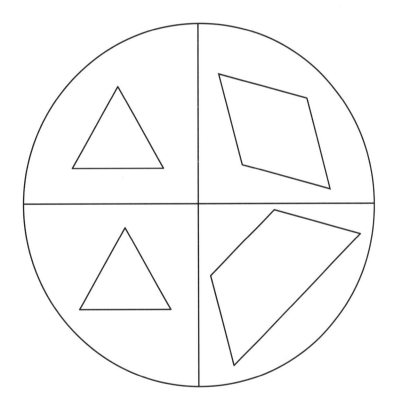

TOY _____   PRICE _____

- -

TOY FACTORY PRICE LIST

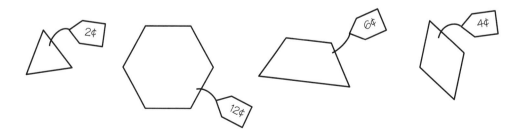

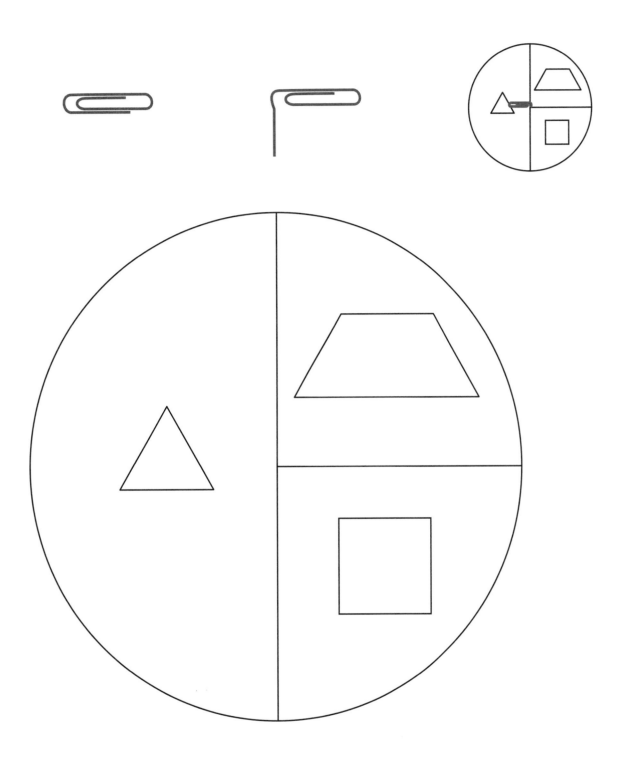

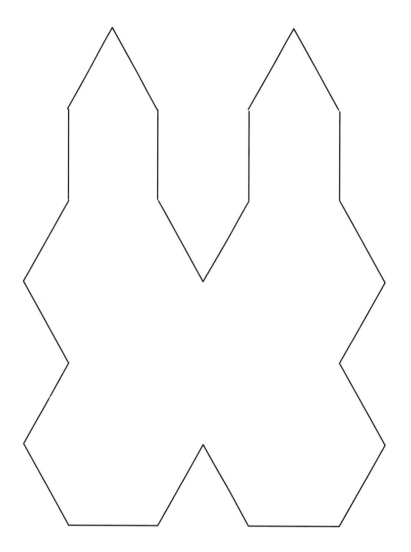

©ETA/Cuisenaire®

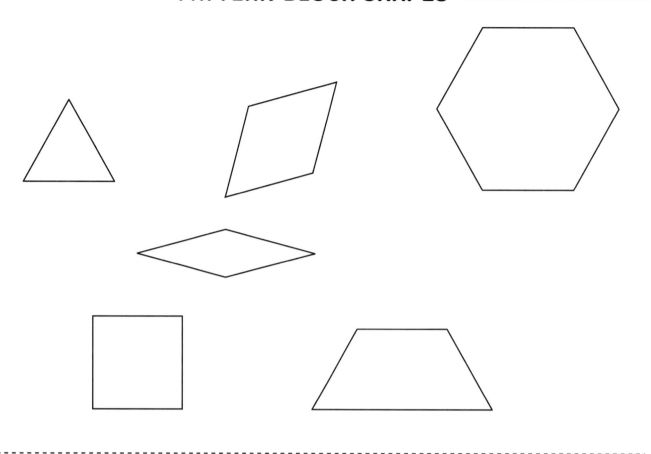

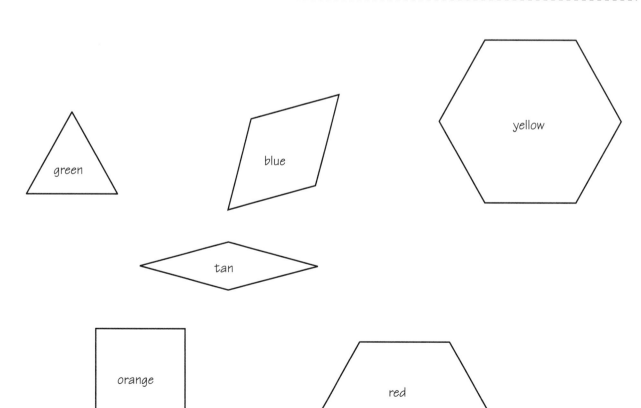

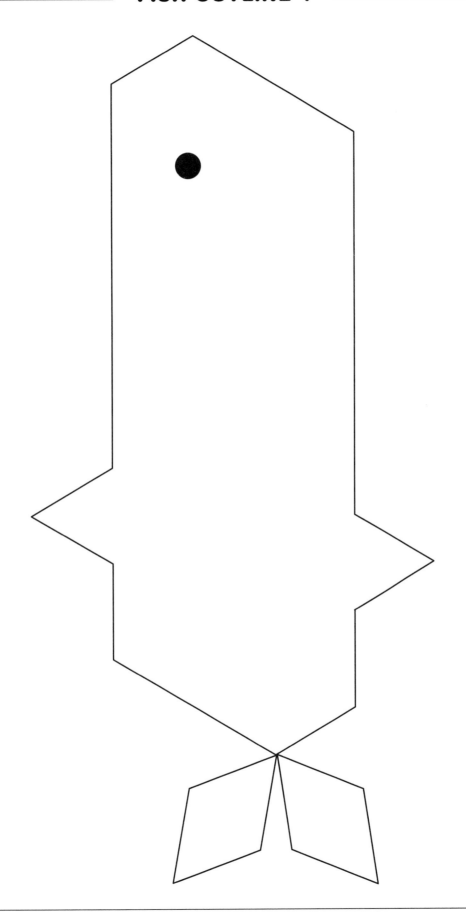

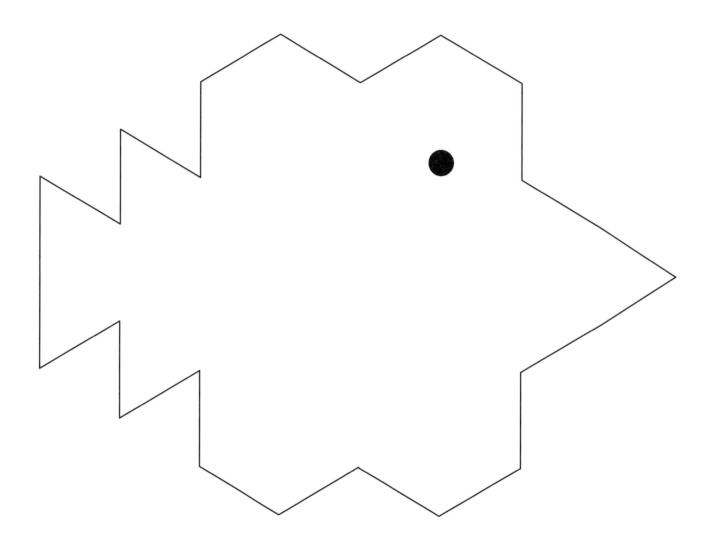

©ETA/Cuisenaire®

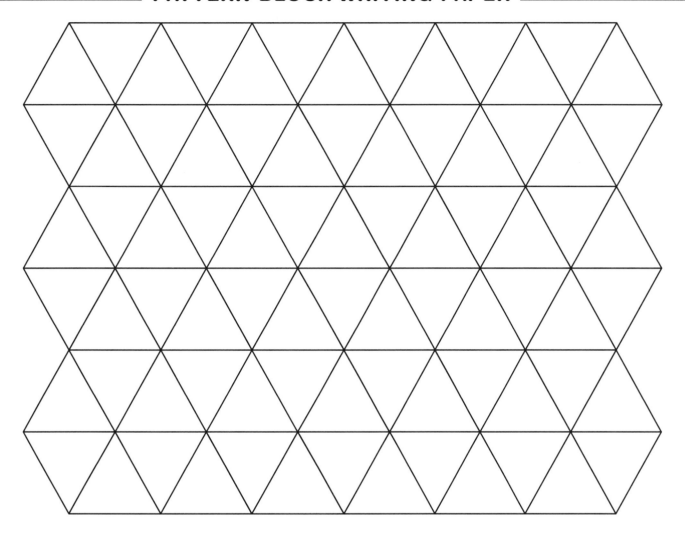

_____

_____

_____

_____

_____

_____

_____

©ETA/Cuisenaire®